AF323232

PORTRAIT OF AN EXPATRIATE

William Gardner Smith, 1973

PORTRAIT OF AN EXPATRIATE

William Gardner Smith, Writer

LeRoy S. Hodges, Jr.

Contributions in Afro-American and African Studies, Number 91

Greenwood Press

Westport, Connecticut • London, England

Library of Congress Cataloging-in-Publication Data

Hodges, LeRoy S.
Portrait of an expatriate.

(Contributions in Afro-American and African studies, ISSN 0069-9624 ; no. 91)
Bibliography: p.
Includes index.
1. Smith, William Gardner, 1927-1974. 2. Authors, American—20th century—Biography. 3. Afro-Americans—Biography. I. Title. II. Series.
PS3537.M8685Z69 1985 813′.54 [B] 85-934
ISBN 0-313-24882-6

Library of Congress Catalog Card Number: 85-934
ISBN: 0-313-24882-6
ISSN: 0069-9624

First published in 1985

Greenwood Press
A division of Congressional Information Service, Inc.
88 Post Road West, Westport, Connecticut 06881

Printed in the United States of America

The paper used in this book complies with the Permanent Paper Standard issued by the National Information Standards Organization (Z39.48-1984).

P

In order to keep this title in print and available to the academic community, this edition was produced using digital reprint technology in a relatively short print run. This would not have been attainable using traditional methods. Although the cover has been changed from its original appearance, the text remains the same and all materials and methods used still conform to the highest book-making standards.

Copyright Acknowledgments

Grateful acknowledgment is given for permission to reprint the following:

Extracts from "The Expatriate Tradition 'Then and Now,' " *The Paris Review*, Winter-Spring 1965 issue, No. 33., pp. 158-59, 164-66.

Excerpts reprinted by permission of Farrar, Straus and Giroux, Inc., from: LAST OF THE CONQUERORS, copyright © 1948 by William Gardner Smith; ANGER AT INNOCENCE, copyright © 1950 by William Gardner Smith; SOUTH STREET, copyright © 1954 by William Gardner Smith; and THE STONE FACE, copyright © 1963 by William Gardner Smith.

Excerpts from RETURN TO BLACK AMERICA, copyright © 1970. Reprinted by permission of the publisher, Prentice-Hall, Inc., Englewood Cliffs, NJ 07632.

Reprinting of "The Compensation for the Wound," appearing in *Two Cities*, Summer 1961, pp. 67-69, with the permission of Jean Fanchette.

Correspondence between Jerry H. Bryant and William Gardner Smith and LeRoy S. Hodges, Jr., with the permission of Jerry H. Bryant.

Correspondence between Richard Gibson and LeRoy S. Hodges, Jr., with the permission of Richard Gibson.

Correspondence between Edith Smith Earle, William Gardner Smith, and LeRoy S. Hodges, Jr., with the permission of Edith Smith Earle.

Conversations and excerpts therein and materials given to LeRoy S. Hodges, Jr., by Mary Sewell Smith concerning William Gardner Smith and Mary Sewell Smith with her permission.

Letters and excerpts therein of correspondence between William Gardner Smith, LeRoy S. Hodges, Jr., and Celia Hornung Sanders with her permission.

Every reasonable effort has been made to trace the owners of copyright materials in this book, but in some instances this has proven impossible. The publishers will be glad to receive information leading to more complete acknowledgments in subsequent prints of this book, and in the meantime extend their apologies for any omissions.

IN MEMORIAM

For my loving parents,

Mabel Louise Featherstone Hodges

and LeRoy Samuel Hodges, Sr.

"I am a roving expatriate. . . . I have wandered from place to place, from country to country. . . . I still have no idea where I shall eventually strike roots. . . . This rootlessness has its inconveniences, but it has an advantage, too: it gives a certain perspective. . . . I sailed to Europe for a vacation. This stretched into months, then years. . . ."

—William Gardner Smith, in his
unpublished manuscript,
"Through Dark Eyes"

"The danger of being an expatriate is that you are very likely to find yourself living, in effect, nowhere. . . . This means that, as time goes on, the expatriate may find that he has no real or relevant concerns, and no grasp of reality. He is living, really, on the hazzards and energies of other people; he has ceased to pay his way."

—James Baldwin, in an interview
in Istanbul, Ernest Dunbar, *The
Black Expatriates*, p. 19

Contents

Acknowledgments

This biography of William Gardner Smith could not have been written without the splendid cooperation of many people. In the many hours they granted me for interviews, I came to know Smith, the man, and his career. The research for this study has taken me primarily to Philadelphia, Pennsylvania, and Paris, France, where, in both cities, members of his family and friends welcomed my decision to examine him.

My kindest and warmest regards must begin with Mrs. Edith Earle, his mother, and with Edna and Sydney, Smith's late aunt and younger half sister, who made me feel at home on my many visits to their South Philadelphia residence. Phyllis, his other half sister, was delightful and charming in her remembrance of her half brother. Mary Sewell Smith, his first wife, was extremely kind in recalling her life with him. Solange Royez, Smith's second wife, was a bit apprehensive and cautious, yet answered my probing question of the seventeen years she knew him. And, especially to Ira Reuben Smith, his widow, for her generous outpouring of insights in his failing years, my ongoing deep admiration.

From the initial stages of the research I was rewarded by having an adviser, friend, and mentor James Arthur Miller of Trinity College, Hartford, Connecticut; I hope this work repays, however slightly, my debt to him and reflects my profound respect.

Personal and special regards to Michel Fabre of the Sorbonne Nouvelle, who permitted my utilizing materials in his personal collection of Richard Wright that I knew to be rare or thought to be nonexistent, and to his wife Geneviève of the Université de Paris, for their collective friendship.

Others have given their time and effort in gathering data for inclusion in this study. While some are desirous of remaining anonymous—which, of course, I shall respect—my thanks to them for their contributions. My special appreciation to, in America: Maya Angelou and her secretary Sel Berkowitz, Howard and Mirian Brodsky, Jerry H. Bryant, Joseph Bevans Bush,

Heather Chisholm Chait, Hodee W. Edwards, Edward Field, Kristin Hunter, Wendell Jeanpierre, Ben Johnson, Pyke Johnson, Leslie Alexander Lacy, Robert Lasson, Pamela Oline, Arthur Orrmont, Evelyn Shefner, Layna Verin, Alice Windom, and Robert Wohlforth of Farrar, Strauss & Giroux, Inc,; and, in Europe: Pierre Doublet, Jean Fanchette, Richard Gibson, Beverly Gordey, Katia Grotkamp, Musy Hafner, the late Chester Himes, Jan Kristiansen, Herb Lottman, the late Clara Malraux, the late Julian Mayfield, Bernard and Joan Redmont, Sylvie Shashahani, and Ellen Wright. My warm gratitude to Celia Hornung Sanders, who resides in Australia. Kudos to Seymour Krim.

Further, I want to acknowledge Minerva Katz of the Brooklyn College Library and Ruth Miller of the State University of New York at Stony Brook; Barbara Gessula, Doug Dacres, Pedro J. Figueroa, Thomas Tharpe, and Ron McFarland for their friendship and support; Harry Goldberg of the American Library in Paris; the staff of the Schomburg Collection of the New York City Public Library; and the Beinecke Rare Book and Manuscript Library at Yale University for their cooperation in this undertaking. My thanks to Farrar, Straus & Giroux, Inc., and Prentice-Hall, Inc., for the use of quotations from Smith's works. I am very grateful to Charles D. Moorer for the manuscript preparation.

Finally, to my daughter Heather—"Missy"—with whom I missed so much time in my desire to do this study, this work is especially dedicated.

Introduction

Why devote time and effort researching the life of an expatriate, more specifically, a Black expatriate, when his creative output is considered marginal? Moreover, is a minor writer—as some view him—who permanently departs his native soil worthy of an extended study?

In this first critical biography of William Gardner Smith, the complete man is examined via family, friends, and associates, with particular attention paid to his published and unpublished works. Each book is subjected to an extended summary and scrutinized in detailed fashion that closes with comments of literary critics of the era.

In early November 1974, Smith, born in Philadelphia, Pennsylvania, and longtime resident of Paris, died in France. His presence there began in late 1951, and with a year and a half gap, time spent in Africa, it remained his home for over twenty-three years. What began, in his words, as a "possible year abroad," moved on to "I like the life of Europe" within in two years, to a desk editor [position] at the Agence France-Presse [the French news agency]" after three years, and to a final, "I shall not stay in the States . . . . I shall live outside of [America]."

William Gardner Smith was the author of five books; he claimed to have written ten. In present hindsight, his twenty-year association with Agence France-Presse (AFP) could have been detrimental to his growth as the writer he envisioned himself to be. Actually, within the time span at AFP, he published only two books, a novel and a nonfiction work. But his critical eye and ear retained ongoing news events in his thoughts as stories to be further explored. This, though, would speak only to Smith's artistic output; what about the man's life and career in a foreign land?

The research for answers led to America's federal agencies; the agency whose files produced the most detailed information was the Federal Bureau of Investigation. They began collecting data on Smith just after his departure to Europe, and the work continued through August 1984 when they curtly stated: "This concludes the processing of your information."

Requests to other agencies produced varying responses. The Central Intelligence Agency (CIA) responded to my request by stating: "The cost estimate for us to research for records regarding William Gardner Smith comes to a total of $211." The Department of State saw fit to forward thirty-eight pages of material concerning Smith. The US Department of Justice, Office of the Associate Attorney General, sent a 1970 newspaper article that was an excerpt from Smith's Return to Black America.

In the FBI and State Department documents, names of informers and other information were deleted, causing considerable correspondence with both agencies. The materials released, however, proved informative in an "official" manner.

In the end, Smith's life and career as expatriate and writer seemed to have been lived exactly as he wanted it, with few exceptions. His personal commitment not to reside on his native soil is a fact; but to quote him exactly: "The black man, no matter how long he lived in Europe, drifted through those societies and eternal 'foreigner' among eternal strangers."

The importance of Smith, then, to answer the questions posed at the outset, does not rest solely with his status as an expatriate or as a writer, but is a combination of both.

Chronology

1927 William Gardner Smith born, February 6, to Edith Smith in Philadelphia, Pennsylvania.

1934 Edith Smith marries Douglas Stanley Earle in Philadelphia. Half sister Phyllis born.

1936 Half sister Sydney born.

1938 Half brother, Douglas, Jr., born.

1943 Begins journalism position at the *Pittsburgh Courier*, a Black newspaper in Philadelphia.

1946 Drafted into United States Army. Departs for European tour of duty as occupation soldier in Germany.

1947 Discharged for military service. Completes first novel. Attends Temple University, Philadelphia.

1948 *Last of the Conquerors* published. Becomes engaged to Mary Sewell.

1949 Begins work on new novel. Marries Mary. Terminates studies at Temple.

1950 *Anger at Innocence* published.

1951 Sails to France with Mary.

1952 Mary returns to Philadelphia. Smith remains in Paris, writing new novel.

1953 Completes new novel and begins writing another novel.

1954 *South Street* published. Secures journalistic position with Agence France-Presse in Paris. "Simeon" manuscript completed. Starts new novel.

1957 Marriage ends in divorce. Meets Solange Royez, a French college student.

1959 Begins writing "Pink Ballets."

1960 Completes "Pink Ballets." Plans to write sequel to *Last of the Conquerors*.

1961 Starts new novel. Marries Solange Royez in Paris.

1963 Publication of *The Stone Face*. A daughter, Michele, born in Paris.

1964 With family, leaves Paris to accept post of assistant editor-in-chief of Ghana Television in Accra.

1965 A son, Claude, born in Accra. Becomes director of

	Ghana's Institute of Journalism.
1966	Ghana government overthrown by military coup. Smiths ordered to leave Ghana. Returns to Paris and rejoins Agence France-Presse as a senior editor.
1967	Appointed editor-in-chief of the English Language service of AFP. Returns to America for first time in sixteen years, remains a month, and returns to Paris. Begins writing nonfiction book of expatriate's view of America after many years abroad.
1968	Stepfather dies. Meets Ira Reuben. Separated from Solange.
1970	*Return to Black America* published. Marriage to Solange ends in divorce. Marries Ira Reuben in Paris.
1971	A daughter, Rachel, born in Paris.
1972	Begins writing new book.
1973	Stricken with cancer.
1974	Dies of cancer, November 5, in Thiais, France.

PORTRAIT OF AN EXPATRIATE

Growing up in South Philadelphia 1

The society that William Gardner Smith was born into in Philadelphia, Pennsylvania, on February 6, 1927, was marked by Black progress described as "very gradual from indentured servant to ghetto freedman."[1] Historically, "black people [had] been a significant part of Phildelphia life since the city began in the early seventeenth century. Initially . . . Negro slaves were treated much the same as white indentured slaves. Only after 1700 were laws passed in the city to distinguish the African slave from all other kinds of people . . . [and] the Black population of Philadelphia at the middle of the eighteenth century was estimated to be about 6,000."[2] In a cursory sense, Philadelphia, although, a Northern city, was plagued by the same attitudes and general views concerning Blacks as were the border and Southern states. But Blacks were in Philadelphia to stay and "by 1930, 222,504 Blacks lived in the city."[3] When Smith was eight, the Commonwealth enacted Public Laws 297 and 1173, designed to improve the conditions among Blacks in the City of Brotherly Love.[4]

The Commonwealth was not without its sordid racist past. Conditions affecting Blacks around the turn of the century were reflected in three lynchings in Pennsylvania during a twenty-year period from the spring of 1891 to the summer of 1911. On May 23, 1891, Dennis Hampton of Barnsley was lynched; on December 13, 1899, David Pearce of Dunbar; and on August 13, 1911, Zachariah Walker of Coatesville.[5]

Meanwhile, the voting Blacks in Philadelphia at the time of Smith's birth were Republicans, since, as a group, their memory told them that "the Republicans . . . had restored the franchise to Negroes and . . . the Democrats ruled the racist South."[6] Blacks began a slight change in their voting pattern the following year with more Blacks voting for Democratic candidates in the subsequent years: "In 1932 the Democrats got 30 percent of the Black vote, while getting 42 percent of the city-wide vote."[7] But Blacks were carefully sizing up both political parties for their own advantage. How the Republicans of

Philadelphia were almost driving Negroes from their party during the 1930s can best be illustrated by the following:

> The Republican organization . . . treated . . . [the Negroes] with about as much consideration as the "safe" voting habits required. . . . . Marshall Shepard, a Negro clergyman in Philadelphia . . . recalls once when he and other . . . Negro spokesmen traveled to the Atlantic City summer home of the great William Vare [long-time powerful Republican] to request Negro representation on the GOP ticket for that year. [Vare] replied, according to Shepard: "Never! Never! The [white] people of Philadelphia would never stand [for] it!"[8]

The view of Philadelphia politics concerning its Black citizens during the late 1920s and the early 1930s was important not only to an isolated few, but to scores of Blacks and liberal whites who were well aware of abuses based solely on race. The overall scene in the City of Brotherly Love would continue to claim its victims of racial discrimination in many ways. Within the following decade William Gardner Smith would become another senseless victim.

On May 13, 1934, Edith Smith and Douglas Stanley Earle were married at St. Simon Episcopal Church in Philadelphia. Officiating was the Reverend John Logan, Sr. Earle, born in Cambridge, Maryland, was of medium height, energetic, quiet, a rather unassuming man. He was employed at the Abbott Milk Company as a custodian.[9]

The Earles moved to 1424 South 19th street, where, on October 9, Mrs. Edith Earle gave birth to a daughter, Phyllis. Young William Gardner Smith, now almost eight years old, immediately took to the baby. He would rock Phyllis to sleep, help to feed her, play with her, and always try to please their mother. However, he did not like his stepfather, although, his young mind could not be sure as to why. A slow-growing dislike developed for his stepfather, a dislike that would last for years. To Earle, young Smith was "his" son, whom he treated with fatherly disposition. But to Smith, Earle was not his real father. He began, possibly at this tender point in his life, to increase his distance, subconsciously, from his stepfather. In later years, in a reflective mood, he would talk about the situation with several people. Smith "had problems with his stepfather," one person would say.[10] However, "he felt a deep affection for his mother [and] . . . was, in fact . . . love with her."[11]

Less than two years later, on August 17, 1936, a second half sister named Sydney, was born at the University of Pennsylvania Hospital. Smith, now nine, could continue playing, cleaning up, and cuddling his two sisters with great affection. He was now attending Walter George Smith Public School on Warton and South 19th Streets and could not wait to get home from school to look after them. He took on a protective—fatherly?—attitude towards the "kids," as he was later to call them. Some unseen force seemed to advance Smith beyond his tender years. Race relations had been introduced to him a couple of years earlier:

> I must [have] been 7 or 8 . . . and it was in the history class. . . . at school. The story of Capt. John Smith and Pocahontas came up, and the teacher remarked that John Smith "lost caste" by marrying the Indian girl. I immediately raised my hand and wanted to know how he lost caste when he was just a captain while she was a real princess? The teacher hemmed and hawed, and I remember being confused and for the first time in my life very depressed. I went home wondering about castes and why I had to be someone different—a Negro.[12]

Smith thus pinpoints the incident as the time when the "problem" first struck him.

In 1938 eleven-year-old William Gardner Smith, excellent student that he was, found himself anticipating which classes he would attend in the fall of that year. Still the "little man" in the family, he continued caring for his sisters and was as eager as his mother for the arrival of the new baby. Four-year-old Phyllis and two-year-old Sydney did not understand why their mother went to the University of Pennsylvania Hospital in late October; Smith, however, knew and was secretly pleased.

On October 26 the Earles were joyous when Edith gave birth to their son, Douglas, Jr. Bill Smith as extremely happy—a half brother! But he kept to himself his ongoing dislike of his stepfather. Certain things were becoming clearer. He understood that the union of his mother and stepfather had produced Douglas, Jr.—who was nicknamed "Sonny"—and Phyllis and Sydney. But Earle was not <u>his</u> father. Who was?[13] His sisters and brother took up most of his time, along with the homework given by the teachers at school.

Smith seems to have overcome his deeper thoughts by wearing a mask, as it were, appearing only as a bright, normal, intelligent child. Other children found school a bore, something to put up with until they finished one way or another; he was the complete opposite. The Walter George Smith Public was, during this period, "a very fine school where everyday we learned of the contributions made by Black people to the making and shaping of this country", Smith later remembered, "a school where the only thing white was chalk—all Black teachers, students and a Black principal, Mr. George Lyles. . . . (many years later [it] became [known] that this had been a pilot program designed to test the capacity of [Black people] to run a Philadelphia public school)."[14]

By 1940 Smith was attending the Barratt Junior High School. Excellent grades were now commonplace for him. Barratt was located four blocks east and two blocks north of the 1828 Wilder Street residence the Earles now lived in. The junior high school was attended mostly by Black youngsters from South Philadelphia. There Smith was to meet an excellent group of teachers who recognized the talent he possessed. On October 15, 1940, his IQ was measured and registered 122, an extremely high score.[15] And he was becoming the neighborhood "storyteller," concocting tales to the amusement and amazement of younger children. By now he had the appearance of a "skinny (almost frail), scholarly-looking . . . budding writer [who] would speak of books . . . by [Richard] Wright and [Ernest] Hemingway . . . whom he read and . . . admired."[16] But it was also a time, Smith wrote, when "at the age of nine I went to work in a grocery store at two dollars a week . . . and remember from those days the sight of Negro boys pulling home on wagons relief supplies from the nearest station. At the age of 13 I went to work at a photographic studio, and learned the business."[17] Further, he recalled:

> The days before the Second World War, in the day before the other children were born: how my cousins and I used to stuff wads of newspaper into our shoes to keep our feet from touching the ground through the holes in our soles; how fire, touched off by the toppling of a rickety oil stove, had burned down a house, a firetrap, in which we lived, destroying many of our belongings; how we slept in our underwear, four to a bed, two beds to the tiny room; how we all went to work early in life . . . to supplement the family income. How we all pulled together, a clan dominated by the strong spirit of my grandmother, turning our earnings over to the family so that the family, as a unit, could survive.[18]

The day before Smith's fourteenth birthday, having completed Barratt Junior High School, he entered Benjamin Franklin High School, at a distance from Wilder Street, on 13th and Green Streets in North Philadelphia. It has been said that "excellent teachers produce excellent students" and, if that statement has merit, Smith was a prize example of such process. In particular, he enjoyed modern fiction, mostly Hemingway and [William] Faulkner, although he read whatever interested him at the moment, including the "New Republic and The Nation magazines."[19] It is interesting to note that he had, "at the age of 11 . . . read all of Hemingway's works up to that time, and also an awful lot of [William Somerset] Maugham. In the next few years [he] was impressed by [Marcel] Proust (for his poetic allusions) and [Fëdor] Doestoevski (for his intensity)."[20]

Smith was now standing five feet eight, weighing about 130 pounds. Growth in a poor Black community, other than physical, is often premature, necessary for survival, and a fact of life. Girls, many in their early teens, give birth to children; young boys in most cases the fathers, experience a need to live every moment, for what assures a tomorrow? Plans in the ghetto often stretch no longer than the party next weekend; shunting from one situation to the next is almost a normal way of living. Smith described a fictionalized activity that took place in the South Philadelphia ghetto, one in which possibly he was a participant:

The Chase: a game, a sport, an entertainment for simmering evenings when the sun leaned red over the rooftoops and boredom threatened with approaching night. A ball, the key to the game, was tossed lazily back and forth in the street among the sweating boys. . . . .

The tossed ball would seem to float in the air. A girl would dart from the pavement in to the street, leap with hand upstretched in to the air and snatch the ball in flight. Laughing she would then stand between the two groups of boys, holding the ball in her hand, stretching the hand toward them teasingly. "Come and get it, come and get it." Meanwhile, the other girls would have raced up to the end of the street, far beyond the boys. . . . One of the boys would say: "Okay, okay, Sarah, give us the ball." Sarah would laugh. "Come and take it from, if you're big enough!

She would hold the ball temptingly at arm's length. They would come closer, closer and when they were very near Sarah would howl with glee and hurl the ball with all her strength up the street, to the other girls. Laughing in triumph, then, Sarah would dash through the ranks of the boys and run to join the other girls. . . .

In no particular hurry, at an easy trot, the boys would start up the streets towards the girls. Shrieking with delight and fear, the girls kicked up their heels and ran around the corner, onto South Street. The Chase was on. . . .

From time to time the girls, when they could really bear to run no longer, slowed down to a walk. So did the boys. Their aim, now, was not so much to catch the girls as to keep them in sight, keep the distance between them constant. . . . Boy to boy: "That Reety sure is got some fine legs!" Boy to boy: "look at Sarah's nice big jelly-roll ass!" . . .

They would finally reach the outskirts of the city, the endless wasteland of vacant lots covered with twisted grass . . . Here. . . the girls hesitated, dizzy and terrified; wanting to shout for help, to be safe at home, at mother's knee. They turned terror-stricken eyes on the approaching boys, whose frozen smiles belied their trembling legs, the unbearable drumming of their hearts. The boys came on relentlessly.

Turning, in a dream, the girls dashed on the grass, running and screaming, running as though for dear life now, falling, getting up, running again. The lumbering bull-boys ran, too—no longer talking and joking, no longer trying merely to keep the girls in sight, but running in earnest, running to trap and hold and take. . . . The girls cried for help with all their might, but there was no one to hear; their screams rolled out across the wasteland of lots and up to the darkening sky. The foremost boy leaped and tackled the nearest girl, bringing her roughly to the ground. One by one

> each of the girls felt hungry hands seize her and hold her and throw her to the grass. There were not enough girls for all the boys. No matter: two boys could take one girl.
>
> What always followed, though not precisely rape, had always seemed like rape. . . . The girls kicked and clawed and punched and bit. The boys held them fast, forcing their dresses up and their drawers down. Exhausted, overpowered, the girls were taken one by one. Nightfall, and strange sounds in the silence of the twisted grass. Sweat mingling with sweat. Eventually it was over.[21]

Some young people living in the ghetto do plan beyond tomorrow or next weekend, even though one is never promised today.

While at Benjamin Franklin High School, Smith also participaed in a large number of school-related activities. And while almost living in two different worlds—one good, the other questionable—Smith, "along with other boys from the area, would sneak on the Broad street Subway on Sundays and ride up and down Snyder to Olney, a big outing for young Black kids growing up down in South Philly in those tough times."[22] In later years he would reflect on this period:

> In the social and spiritual misery of the ghetto, the gangs, like wolf packs, sprouted as though by spontaneous generation. Summers in South Philadelphia, we poured on into the streets, out of our overcrowed homes, onto Wilder Street . . . not knowing what to do with ourselves, for there were no playgrounds, no organized amusements, and we had no money. . . . The kids played half-ball or deadbox or baseball with a rubber ball. . . . The difficulties came with the night, when the youths were reluctant to return to the stifling rooms and the narrow beds where . . . they slept . . . in their underwear, waking frequently during the night to brush the bedbugs away. We gathered on the corner . . . hating the white cops who passed continually in their patrol cars, ordering us to "get off the corner," sometimes calling us niggers; and hating, also, the entire encompassing world, the black and the white; hating the black because it lived in this moldering, lightless, humiliating, dreamless, scorpion pit; the white because it lived so well, with light and laughter and money and carelessness and condescension and prestige, and was responsible, somehow, we were not sure, for the way we lived. It was a fearful world: if you ventured beyond your particular neighborhood, in the Italian or the Irish quarters, for example, you were inevitably attacked and beaten or worse; if you went to North or West Philadelphia, to the kingdoms of the Northsiders or the Tops or the Bottoms, you were attacked and beaten by blacks. It was normal to think in terms of defense, normal to think in terms of vengeance, thus normal to

> form the local knights of the round table, a gang: cocoon, womb, and mailed fist. We named ours the Roaches.[23]

In the early 1940s South Philadelphia was a brutal place for anyone to grow, develop, or live. Smith, like untold thousands, would carry the psychological scars he received there indefinitely. But he went through this period without a physical mark on his frame.

It was his last year in high school when he met Mary Sewell, one of the few Black girls who attended Girl's High School, a predominately white school during that period. They had met at a party during the summer of 1943.[24] The initial meeting was followed by future encounters at other parties, after-school walks, and movie dates. Meanwhile, World War II was in progress and Smith, now sixteen, was moving toward draft status.

One of his teachers, Dr. Gerald Hamm, a white English instructor at Benjamin Franklin High School, is credited with encouraging Smith to become a writer; the school principal, Charles H. Williams, was to contact the editor of a weekly newspaper and recommend him for a possible position.[25] In his English classes Smith's grades were straight A for the six terms at Franklin; his first-and second-year French language grades averaged C, while his typing classes gave him another A.[26] At Franklin, now nicknamed Smitty, he was extremely active in school activities. The school's yearbook would list his accomplishments:

> [He] was the captain of our championship fencing team. He was a real Franklin rooter from the day he arrived from Barratt. He loves photography and has an unquenchable thirst for literature. He was a good cheerleader. Bill was also editor of the school paper, The Junto, and of our yearbook, The Almanac. As a judge of the Student Court, he was a pillar of justice. Smitty wants to have a career as a writer, after he finishes college.
>
> Activities: Captain Fencing Team, cheerleader, Student Court, Editor of Junto, Editor of Almanac, Delegate-at-Large to Student Council, English Club, Student Patrol, Camera Club.[27]

In January 1944, at age sixteen Smith graduated with honors as the second-highest student in a class of seventy-four.[28] He refused scholarships to Howard and Lincoln Universities, believing that he could learn more about writing by being a journalist.[29]

The Pittsburgh Courier, one of the big three Black newspapers of Smith's youth, had been published since 1910. The Courier enabled young Blacks to read and meet such columnists as Benjamin Mays, J. A. Rogers, George S. Schuyler, and P. L. Prattis. Its cirulation was nationwide, and it went into Black school libraries and colleges. Like the Baltimore-based

Afro-American and Chicago's Defender, it had a profound influence on the thinking of young Black Americans and maintained a bureau office in Philadelphia. In 1944 the editor of the office was J. Austin Norris, and the weekly had a large circulation in the Black communities of Pennsylvania as well as the adjoining states of Maryland, Ohio, and New Jersey. The readership was loyal and the newspaper's growth was steadily increasing, possibly because of the Courier's closely following the Black men in the military and their actions on both the European and Asian war fronts. Black demands for equality in the armed forces and civilian racial grievances were duly reported. John A. Saunders, city editor of the Philadelphia bureau of the Pittsburg Courier, remembered Smith: "Bill came to see me at the office of the [newspaper] when I was city editor, and told me he wanted a job. He was a senior at Ben Franklin High at the time, and had brought with him several articles he had written for the school newspaper. After reading one of the articles by Bill, I offered him a full-time job after he finished school and a part-time job, if he wanted it, while he was still in school. He accepted the part-time job and later the full-time job."[30]

Smith began working full-time during February 1944 after graduation from Franklin.[31] His assignments were to investigate stories that Saunders deemed important. They worked together, youngster Smith learning from the veteran newspaperman. And as a team they worked real well, Smith totally engrossed in his work. The long hours meant nothing; he was learning the art of reporting extremely well through Saunders' guidance. Thus time was only a word, had no meaning for Smith. At eighteen he had been working for a little over a year at the Courier. His girlfriend, Mary Sewell, was proud of him; this young man was on the rise. Joseph Bevans Bush, Smith's boyhood friend says, "I recall him writing a story on my brother, Mussy (Gerald Whitaker Bush) who had graduated from Barratt Junior High School with top scholastic honors for which he was awarded a trophy by a group of South Philly businessmen."[32] Constantly busy writing for the paper, Smith had periods when social occasions had to be placed second. In a letter apologizing for not being present at a Benjamin Franklin High School event, he wrote to the principal:

> I am very sorry I was not very I was not able to attend the alumni banquet last week, but when I received the letter announcing that one was to be held, I expected it to be at an hour later than it was.
>
> As things turned out, it was not only held too early for me to attend, but it was also held on the deadline night of our weekly paper. I did not finish work until 8:30 o'clock, and I would have had to dress before attending.
>
> Enclosed you will find $2.00 for the cost of the meal. But I really regret not seeing the fellows again. I'll come up to the school before I leave for the Merchant Marines.[33]

Smith did not join the Merchant Marine. On May 8, 1945, Germany surrendered and the war ended in Europe; it continued, however, in the Far East. All eyes looked to Japan when, on August 6, America dropped its first atomic bomb on Hiroshima. Seventy-two hours later the second A-bomb was dropped on Nagasaki. The ensuing holocaust forced Japan to surrender. Formal proceedings were finalized on August 14, 1945, when the treaty ending the war with Japan was signed. American involvement in war in Europe and the Pacific was over; the Second Great War had ended.

Smith received his letter of induction into the US Army in early December 1945. The stunned family fell silent for a moment, but the next instant was filled with "Well, the war's over anyway!" "Maybe the government will reconsider since Bill's a reporter." "It's probably a mistake!" All hopes were dashed within a month. On January 8, 1946, Smith was drafted. It was a typical midwinter day when he arrived at Fort George G. Meade, Maryland, outside Baltimore, after a bus trip of almost three hours. Shortly thereafter, he was transferred to Fort Leonard Wood, Missouri.

The first month and a half rushed by, culminating with his qualifying as Marksman on the rifle range on February 26.[34] Completing basic training, he was placed on orders with the destination ETO—European theater of operations. Returning to Philadelphia on a furlough during May, he relaxed visiting neighbors and going out on dates. On one particular date he "took a girl friend to a night club. Although she was Negro her skin was so light that she was often mistaken for white, and this caused a disturbance that evening. A group of [white] sailors in uniform closed in on [Smith] and beat him up badly while others in the place took up the cry: 'Kill him! Kill him.'"[35] After the incident Smith said, "I felt then and there that I should hate every white person who ever lived, but I just couldn't. I have too many white friends whom I know and respect and the feeling is reciprocated."[36]

Furlough completed, he sailed to Europe on June 1. The troopship crossed the Atlantic in nonrecord time, arriving on June 13. After a train and truck ride to the replacement depot, he was assigned to the 661st TC Truck Company, as a clerk-typist, in Berlin."[37] Still taking everything in stride, he was now an occupation soldier in war-torn and devastated Germany. His assignment was summed up briefly in his official military records: "Served . . . as clerk typist . . . worked in the Orderly Room. Kept the records in good condition. Made out Morning Reports. Also was in charge of Motor Pool employing 76 Germans."[38] This statement typifies the military account of Smith's <u>formal</u> discharge of duties. What <u>personal</u> changes he was <u>to undergo</u> was an entirely <u>different story</u>. He was to serve a total of eight months and one day in Europe, including the time spent traveling from and back to America. The tour of duty, the sights, the people—everything was to be remembered by Smith. As he embarked on the return trip to America, he recalled, "It was very stormy and I was dizzy and seasick. . . . As I was editor of the ship's paper and had a little office and typewriter, I started typing aimlessly to distract myself. It was blind, inane stuff at first and I kept pecking out: 'You can so write. Now is the time. Now is the time. Now. Right now.' I kept doing that till the real words came and the book got started."[39]

The Liberty Ship SS Marine Robbin arrived in New York harbor on February 1, 1947, and Smith, along with the other soon-to-be-civilians, was taken to Fort Dix, New Jersey, where he was honorably discharged on February 19.[40] With the $169.80 given him at the separation center, Smith was once again a civilian and on his way home to his family and Mary.[41] He was elated being home again and enjoyed himself for several days. Then picking up the notes typed aboard ship, he began writing through most nights until August. The book took shape and he "finished it on the kitchen table . . . eight months in all."[42] During this period the only financial support he had was the small allotment he earned under the GI bill for attending Temple University; he had been a full-time student there since March 8.[43]

Early in September, Smith wrote to many publishers, including Farrar, Straus and Company. His letters gave a story line, suggesting the novel's content, and he received a response stating that they would be glad to read the manuscript. The title Smith had selected was "Dark Tide over Deutschland."[44] Farrar, Straus and Company were very interested. On the morning of October 27 they sent the following telegram: "We want to publish your novel. Suggest you ring Murray Hill 3-4830 collect. Regards. John Farrar."[45]

Smith was thrilled and his family extremely proud; Mary was completely happy. A party was held that evening at the family home on Wilder Street. Then on October 31 the publishing company wrote: "Here is the contract, drawn along the lines which we discussed. I hope you will find it in order. . . . If it is in order, return one copy, signed, to me for our files and a check for $500 will be sent to you. . . . It's good to have you as an author."[46]

Correspondence continued between the publisher and Smith with the letters questioning the title of the novel. By early December, Smith had changed the title. John Farrar, writing to Smith, said: "Thanks for sending me on the best-seller list. At quick glance, THE HAMMER AND THE NAIL as a title sounds better, certainly, and the idea for the book okay."[47] Still, the newest title was not the final one. Arthur Orrmont, the editor assigned to the novel at Farrar, Straus finally came up with a title agreeable to all. By mid-December, Smith was informed that "Arthur Orrmont has . . . thought of quite a magnificent title. Everybody here seems to like it very much. It is, 'Last of the Conquerors.'"[48] Eight months would pass until Smith received the telegram he undoubtedly longed for: "Happy publication day and all best. John Farrar [and] Roger Straus."[49] In addition, the day was also the birthday of his sister Sydney and Mary. William Gardner Smith, at the age of twenty-one years, six months, and eleven days had officially published his first novel.

Last of the Conquerors is a sensitive first novel concerning Afro-Americans serving in the United States Army as occupation troops in Germany immediately after World War II.[50] The novel deals with a number of soldiers' individual reactions to racism as the white high command in the Army attempts to isolate them in the countryside of war-torn Germany. Many instances of emotional shock fill the pages as the men are scheduled to return home to racial prejudice in America. The irony of not wanting to return is explained by one of the characters, who really speaks for all of them: "I'll always remember the irony of my going away to Germany to find democracy" (p. 238).

A love story is woven throughout the novel between the black protagonist, Hayes Dawkins, and his German girlfriend, Ilse Mueller. Their story is told in very frank terms and dialogue. The novel is a brutal indictment of the United States Army. It enters an arena that had not been explored in the aftermath of World War II.

Last of the Conquerors begins with Hayes Dawkins's arrival in Germany. The two men who arrive with him, the Professor and Randy, are of slight consequence in the earlier portion of the novel. The Professor, a draftee like Dawkins, was a newspaper reporter as a civilian, while Randy is a reenlistee. He is described as having fought in the war and witnessed the sadistic death of one of his friends at the hands of an SS trooper. Randy's immense dislike of the Germans actually begins the novel's many emotional scenes. After he, Dawkins, and the Professor are invited to the enlisted men's club, they invite a couple of German girls to have a drink. Randy makes a sarcastic remark concerning German people. The girl he is with is terribly upset and tells him, "You cannot talk that way." She finds support from another German girl, who tells him not all Germans are the same, as he describes them. When Randy maintains his position, the girl sitting next to him, the angry one, sarcastically describes the Black man's treatment by whites in America. "She felt she was winning. Randy raised his hand and hit the girl hard across the face" (pp. 35-36). The sharp, crisp exchange between them sets the tone of the inner turmoil of the novel's characters. Smith's minute details are extremely engaging as emotions continually build throughout the novel. From harsher moments to lighter passages, Smith maintains the same even writing style.

The love story begins simply enough: Dawkins meets Ilse Mueller in the dispatch office upon arrival at the unit in Berlin. Their casual talks lead her to ask him if he would like to go to Wannsee Beach with her. While at the beach he reflects on another period of his life:

> I had lain on the beach many times, but never before with a white girl. A white girl. Here, away from the thought of differences for a while, it was odd how quickly I forgot it. It had lost importance. Everyone was blue or green or red. No one stared as we lay on the

> beach together, our skins contrasting but our hearts beating identically and both with noses in the center of our faces. Odd, it seemed to me, that here, in the land of hate, I should find this one all-important phase of democracy. And suddenly I felt bitter.[51]

Dawkins's bitterness originates in the American nightmare, manifested by its doctrine of racism. Here, at the beach, the taboo of Black man with a white woman is shattered, and a subtle change begins to occur in him. He is different from most of his fellow soldiers; he is an intellectual. Smith moves the novel at a steady pace, constantly probing deeper conflicts of the characters.

The following week Ilse invites him to meet her aunt and uncle, in whose home she lives. He meets them, and after a brief conversation her relatives retire to their bedroom. Ilse shows him her bedroom, where he sits as she goes into the bathroom. She emerges "wearing a sheer nightgown. She looked surprised because [he] had not undressed" (p. 55). Her surprise possibly stems from the fact that their relationship had moved to this position without Dawkins understanding her feelings toward him. She is not promiscuous, but rather a nice girl with normal desires. Their first night together ends the first section of Last of the Conquerors. Thus, Smith has introduced the love aspect of the story as well as given an indication of the brooding racial elements within the novel.

The company to which Dawkins is assigned is headed by Captain Doyle, the "white-skinned" commanding officer; the balance of the unit is Black. The major theme in the novel is the Black soldiers' lack of enthusiasm for returning to America; one returns unwillingly, and another commits murder, while still others desert. Book Two ends with Dawkins and the Professor being transferred to another part of Germany; the camp they are being assigned to is considered a "nigger hell" and becomes the pivotal setting of the novel. The first sergeant, named Brink, is described as an "Uncle Tom," while Captain Polke, the white commanding officer, is a "cracker" (pp. 129-30).

At the new unit the Black troops are restricted to the camp because several soldiers had contracted venereal disease. Brink is as brutal and sadistic as Polke, and both run the company like a plantation in days of slavery: Polke the slave master, and Brink the "head-nigger-in-charge." Corporal Stevenson, the company clerk, does not like Brink and despises Polke because, as he tells Dawkins, Captain Polke

> "sure hates to see one of the boys with a white girl. He'd rather seen the Germans win the war, no kiddin'. All these officers is the same. . . . That's the way I feel about these white chicks. He said anything to you about them yet?"
>
> "Something about VD."
>
> "Yeah. That's his story. He's had VD twice himself and got treated by a German doctor in town. The doctor talked and now everybody in the town knows about it.

They are all laughing" (pp. 138-39).

Dawkins later befriends McDonald; McDonald's girlfriend listens to Dawkins's complaint of being transferred from Berlin and Ilse. She tells him Ilse will come to him if she really loves him, and in time, after a grueling trip through the Russian and American zones of occupied Germany, Ilse appears. She finds a room with an elderly couple as she and Dawkins continue their romance. Returning home with him from a visit to her uncle, she is taken away from him by the military police for a VD check. The entire scene is racially motivated, but Dawkins can do nothing but watch as the MPs place her in a jeep and drive off (p. 191).

At the camp things grow worse between Brink and Stevenson. Dawkins remembers Stevenson's earlier casual remark that "somebody's gonna shoot both of them one of these days" (p. 137). Meanwhile, with Ilse being held on VD charges, Dawkins's concern for her intensifies. The next morning he "reports the incident of her arrest to Captain Polke, who says he can't do anything."

Two weeks later Ilse is released and explains to her lover the details of her detention. As Dawkins listens, he also reflects on his living among Germans as a man first, color or race being secondary, and on returning to America, which means reverting to a dehumanized role. The idea of his one day living in Germany mounts.

In Book Five, the concluding section, the story becomes extremely complex. It begins with Brink's wanting the names of all the men with low Army General Classification Test scores. The names are being gathered because the company and battalion headquarters expect to give dishonorable discharges to more than half the battalion's fifteen hundred men.

Brink asks Stevenson to make out a statement that will be used to justify each man's discharge; Stevenson tells him he will not comply. Brink informs Captain Polke of his refusal, and Polke orders Stevenson to make out the statement. He resists the order and shortly thereafter is court-martialed. Sentenced to six months in the stockade, he changes dramatically the day after his trial. Although he assures Dawkins he is okay, Stevenson is a crushed and broken man, and he knows Brink and Polke are gleeful.

At home Dawkins tells Ilse he will return to Germany to live. She asks him what motivated his statement. Dawkins responds: "It is like a nail that is driven into a wall. Every blow of the hammer makes it go in further."[52]

Smith now moves the story to its unexpected resolution. Actually there are two situations to be resolved: the Stevenson-Brink-Polke conflict at the camp and Dawkins's involvement with Ilse.

A smoldering resentment fills the orderly room because of recent events, but mostly because of the continued abuse of authority by Brink and Polke. Smith sets the scene for final denouement as Stevenson enters the office with a guard and asks Brink for a copy of his orders. Brink sarcastically tells him he will have ample time to see them from his cell. Stevenson attempts to "reach the sergeant across the desk" to do him bodily harm, but is physically removed from the office. Dawkins returns to work as Brink tells him he is leaving for the dispatch office. Then, abruptly, Dawkins hears an unusual sound.

The sound is that of a carbine being fired. The person firing is Stevenson, whom Dawkins sees outside the captain's window. Stevenson shouts "I'll teach you people to keep messing with me," as he fires more shots into the office. Polke crawls out of his office and barricades the entrance of a room upstairs where he and Dawkins find refuge. Ashamed of himself, Dawkins goes downstairs where he is confronted by Stevenson. He assures Dawkins he "ain't gonna shoot" him; it's the captain he wants: "I got to get that bastard captain. I got the first sergeant. Think I killed him. Now I got to get that captain" (p. 229). Dawkins advises him not to shoot the captain. Stevenson hesitates and finally asks Dawkins to start the motor of a truck parked nearby; he complies as Stevenson runs past him, jumps into the truck, and speeds off. Polke reappears as one of the guards informs him that Brink was shot as well as another sergeant. The captain volunteers to drive the casualties to the hospital; actually he is fearful that Stevenson will return. At the hospital Polke is informed that Brink is dead.

An inquiry is held and Dawkins is questioned. He details the violence of several days earlier. When the interrogation ends, Dawkins returns to work to find that Polke wants to know what transpired. "I don't think the colonel meant for me to broadcast the things he asked," Dawkins tells him (p. 243). The captain then attempts to bribe him the next day by asking: "You want to go to college, don't you?" Dawkins is suspicious; Polke realizes that Dawkins's testimony can damage his military career and concludes their talk on an ominous note. The next morning Dawkins receives a call from battalion headquarters: he is to be court-martialed for missing bed-check, as Polke further attempts to coerce him. He later asks Polke if the education offer still stands; Polke agrees it does.

William Gardner Smith now shows a flaw in Dawkins's character in his succumbing to Polke's insidious plan to remove any possible witness to his dereliction to duty or cowardice in confronting the murderous Stevenson. Rather than face the possibility of a court-martial, Dawkins chooses the easiest way out of the dilemma and gives in to Polke's plan of getting him out of the Army. Dawkins act is nonheroic in light of Stevenson's violent outburst, resulting in Brink's death, or of the other men's expressing their rage by deserting the Army and not returning to America.

Dawkins informs Ilse that his "time is almost up." The next day he is told that he will be shipped home on the following day. Leaving the camp, he goes to Ilse. Ilse breaks the silence by asking him when he will be leaving for America. In this highly emotional scene he cries and can only nod his head in agreement as she senses he will be leaving the next day. In the morning she emotionally shouts at Dawkins: "You will not be back." He is taken aback and tries to be careful, not fully aware of the meaning of the outburst. She continues her tirade. Finally, a thoroughly shaken Dawkins manages to tell her he will return, but something is different in his voice.

After Ilse calms down, they leave the house together and he returns to camp. She waits outside the camp gate as he gathers his belongings and bids farewell to the Professor and other friends. They get aboard a waiting truck and ride to battalion headquarters. The truck stops at the gate and they get off, noticing the soldiers walking leisurely inside the headquarters compound. Dawkins

> . . . gripped Ilse's hand and saw the tears well up in her eyes.
>
> "Until we see each other again, doll baby."
>
> "Goodbye, my Hayes."
>
> She at the gate, duffel bag on my shoulders, walking into the camp. Along the dirt road toward the personnel building. A soldier shouts:
>
> "Say Hayes, I hear you're shipping for home today."
>
> Hoarsely: "Yeah."
>
> "Tough."

Last of the Conquerors ends on the word "Tough," a descriptive adjective for the entire novel.

This ending, the likely end of an affair also takes on significance in that Smith seems to write well beyond his age of twenty. The novel's strength stems from its semi autobiographical aspect: the story appears to be taken from a diary, although he never kept one. Moreover, the novel seems to be an expansion or a fictionalized treatment of an Ebony magazine article titled "Germany Meets the Negro Solider," published less than two years earlier.[53]

The novel derives its power from a penetrating examination of Black soldiers in a racially segregated American Army and is the first twentieth-century novel by an Afro-American writer to deal with this sensitive matter. The illuminating story was received by literary critics of 1948 quite favorably. Jack Conroy wrote in the Chicago Sun Times: "Profanity for its own sake is gratifyingly scarce. The writing for the most part is strong, simple, and lively. One might be tempted to recommend the excision of some parts which are too hortatory or too biased, but it should be realized these artistic defects usually accompany the novel with a bitter message. They are an almost inescapable by-product of the tempestous emotion which brings such works into being."[54] In the Saturday Review of Literature of August 28, 1948, Harrison Smith noted that "Last of the Conquerors will be attacked with considerable venom. It may be entertaining to read what a few southern critics have to say about it, since it violates certain principles held to be true and indivisible, that white and black are not equal, and so should not have the same opportunities, either in life, or in love, or in hope for the future."[55] A Southern critic, Michael Bruen of the Dallas Times Herald, appeared to have accepted Harrison Smith's slightly disguised challenge. Bruen said: "This is a good story and surely true. The author does not have any great style, and humor and geniality are as little evident in the writing as they are in the leading character, but the story does not call for frivolity. It emerges an earnest, honest and bitter novel written with thought-provoking sincerity. Because of its theme and its sincerity it ought not be ignored. It may not be an enjoyable book, but its content is important."[56]

Last of the Conquerors went on to become a brisk seller in 1948.

Writing out of the Ghetto 2

The winter of 1947-48 did not seem as cold to the Earles as had previous winters. In fact, they were delighted now that everything seemed to be coming together; most exciting was that they were now property owners. No more renting places that were close to subhuman living conditions. Their oldest son was now attending Temple University and was a soon-to-be published writer. Thirteen-year-old Phyllis was maintaining excellent grades in school; Sydney, two years younger, was caught up in doing the popular dance of the day, jitterbugging, and in chewing gum and wearing dungarees, bobby socks, and penny loafers. The baby of the family, Sonny, was then nine.

Smith had gotten into a rut while writing Conquerors. He was accustomed to staying up late and had begun writing a new novel. But the early morning classes at Temple, although he could handle them, were in conflict with his writing habits. Being nocturnal, he had to decide where to focus his energies. Would it be college or writing? Rather than decide immediately, he continued classes and writing, and both suffered.

Mary Sewell was also attending Temple, and they were constantly together on and off campus. They were always being invited to various affairs; the publication, by now, of Last of the Conquerors, made him a sort of celebrity in college and in the city. He enjoyed being in the spotlight; it made up, in part, for years of living in the shadows, and he could be most attractive in situations that required grace, dignity, poise, and charm. At Temple he was held in awe by professors and students alike. He would debate varying subjects with skill, the students usually adopting whatever position he took. Meanwhile, Farrar and Straus were sending him letters questioning the development of the next novel.

Smith would often go to New York to get away from Philadelphia. Once there, he'd take in the sights, attend the theater, visit museums, and try to unwind. During one trip he met Canada Lee, an important Black actor of the day. He probably met Lee during February 1949, specifically during

Negro History Week, at the presentation of the Jerome Bowers Peterson Memorial Collection of Photographs of Celebrated Negroes by Carl Van Vechten, at the Music and Art Show at Wadleigh High School on 114th Street in Harlem.[1] It is further probable that he met Mrs. Shirley Graham, who would shortly marry Dr. W. E. B. Du Bois, at the same time; Smith and Graham appeared together at a teachers union conference in Philadelphia on March 5.[2] Canada Lee had appeared in Richard Wright's *Native Son*, a play dramatizing the novel of the same name some years earlier, and was currently appearing in motion pictures. Although Lee was almost twice as old as Smith, they became fast friends. Together they would visit Lee's circle of friends, visits that would last most of any particular night. Somewhere near sunrise Smith would head back to Philadelphia, sleeping on the train en route. The mad scramble would begin once he arrived, trying to get to classes, trying to stay awake, trying to explain his actions to his family and Mary. Free-spirited, he wanted to be with Mary, yet loved roaming around without being responsible to anyone. The realization of time moving on, although he was only twenty-two, the severing of the umbilical cord to home ties, getting his own apartment, a place to write, to study, entertain friends—all were situations that had to be dealt with.

Meanwhile, *Last of the Conquerors* had attracted two New York theatrical producers, T. Edward Hambleton and Alfred Stern. They took an option on the stage rights to produce a dramatization of the novel.[3] The *Temple University News* noted, in an article devoted to Smith, that "stage rights have been bought by two Broadway producers and Bill expects the stage version to be presented next season."[4] The stage version of *Last of the Conquerors*, however, was never produced.

William Gardner Smith and Mary Sewell had, by now, known each other for almost five years. First they were high school sweethearts, then went steady during his apprenticeship as a journalist, corresponded while he was in the Army, and now were attending Temple together. She was always with him; she attended most of his lectures, debates, and appearances in conjunction with the publication of *Last of the Conquerors*. Smith, always outgoing, well-mannered, outspoken on a range of current events and situations, basked in the limelight. Mary, always near, was pleased with the adulation constantly being bestowed on him.

Mary's background was the complete opposite of Smith's. Her father, Dr. Lemuel Sewell, was a practicing physician with a number of years in the field of obstetrics; he had attended Harnamon University in Philadelphia. He had met and married Mary's mother in Philadelphia. They had wanted children almost immediately after marriage. Edward Maxwell Sewell, their only son, was born on May 21, 1923, followed three years later by the birth of Mary on August 17, 1926. A safe, comfortable, excellent educational background usually marks the typical middle-class family: the Sewells enjoyed these comforts without overt pretense. However, when Smith and Mary began seeing each other on a serious level, the Sewells did not know quite how to cope with this youngster from South Philadelphia. They knew the rough neighborhood he lived in—knew it from a safe distance—and wondered why Mary, with her upbringing, would have anything of serious consequence to do with a resident of that area. Her parents thought this was a case of "growing pains" for their daughter and dismissed the relationship as a passing thing. Later, they would openly admire this young man who lived in such a rough and tough neighborhood.

Smith and Mary talked at length with their parents, during the fall and early winter season of 1948, about their getting married. It was decided that a formal announcement would be made before the end of the year. At the Christmas Eve tree trimming in the Sewell home, with several friends in attendance, they announced their engagement with plans for marriage within the next year.[5] The next month, January, 1949, Mary graduated from Temple with a degree in education, majoring in social studies with a minor in English.[6]

The wedding took place on July 23, 1949, at St. Thomas Episcopal Church, 52nd and Parrish Streets, in West Philadelphia. Mary and Bill made an extremely attractive couple. The crowded church held many of their friends, family, and acquaintances. Photographers from the Pittsburgh Courier were there recording the happy event on film; the immediate families were proud of the union. The reception took place at the Sewells' home, and the honeymoon was spent in New York City.

A few days later the young couple moved to 1233 North 54th Street, where they had previously decorated a large one-bedroom apartment. Everything looked wonderful, and they were very happy. Almost immediately, the apartment was constantly filled with various friends, relatives, new faces and personalities. Mary, as a happy, easy-going hostess, enjoyed this period. Smith, always gregarious, inquisitive, welcoming all, marveled at the transition from South 20th Street to the more affluent 54th Street locale.

During this period one of Smith's recent acquaintances, Richard Gibson, a young light-skinned Black, became an almost daily visitor. Gibson, eighteen years old, had met Bill before the wedding and had discussed many subjects with him while a guest at the home of Smith's parents. A person who knew both of them during that period noted "Gibson was raised in poor circumstances by his grandmother, and . . . his father, whom he despised, was a live-in servant to a moderately wealthy Bucks County family."[7] Gibson was attending Kenyon College and was four years younger than Smith; they had been "introduced . . . by a white friend, Mrs. Irene Rose."[8] At the 54th Street apartment they would talk "about politics and every other possible subject under the sun [and] spent hours talking about the art of fiction and techniques of the novel." They "had . . . just read the Notebooks of Henry James and had been greatly impressed by him, who indeed had become for [them] the master. However Bill's original model was Ernest Hemingway. He envied and imitated the terseness of the Hemingway style without falling into parody [but] began to feel . . . that such a style was not ample enough for the complexities he wanted to express." Smith "also read and reread the Russian classics and the French realists from Balzac to Zola. Looking at most Black writers in America . . . he felt that their greatest deficiency was not, as [Gibson] thought in part, of vision, but of style. In particular . . . [they] bemoaned the wooden, Dreiser-esque style of Richard Wright."[9]

When the subject matter would turn to the political scene of the late 1940s, Gibson reflects:

> Politically, Bill was lionized by the Left. He had close contacts with Communists and Trotskyites without sectarianism. This disturbed the CPUSA and he was criticized for his "Trotskyite tendencies," but the fact was he often found the Trots more congenial company as people than the Communists. . . .
>
> It is my conviction that Bill began Marxist-Leninist studies while young, but in an unsystematic fashion. He was approached by the CPSUA and invited to join as a "secret member," but he turned down the offer . . . because he found it difficult to reconcile his personal aesthetic views and the dogmatic socialist realism then preached by the party.[10]

While Smith found stimulation in meeting new people with their varying viewpoints, his academic status at Temple University had terminated at the end of the spring 1949 term, due, in part, to his marriage but mainly to his desire to complete the new novel. At Temple he had garnered a total of sixty-three credits with a grade point average of 3.39 on a 4.00 index.[11] When the apartment was quiet, he busied himself with completing the novel. Meanwhile, Mary, although enjoying the celebrity status of her husband, was beginning to tire slightly of the continual, almost circuslike atmosphere that was becoming a steady routine. Smith, on the other hand, was enjoying the ongoing "show," acquiring a bohemian type of existence that pleased him immensely.

The novel was nearing completion when he suffered the same earlier problem of coming up with a suitable title. Mary thought the title "Rowing in Eden," a line from an Emily Dickinson poem, might be appropriate and Smith agreed with her.[12] His publishers, meanwhile, continued to press him for the manuscript, as they had since early autumn of 1948: "What about that manuscript? I don't want to irritate you but I do want to get it into my hands at the earliest moment that you feel comfortable about it."[13] Included in the letter was this request: "Carl Van Vechten has written asking that you be kind enough to give a telephone call the next time you are in New York. . . . As you know, he has, for many years, made photographing more than a hobby and founded many collections of photographs of prominent Negroes."[14]

As the pace of everything around Smith was increasing, Mary's enthusiam was beginning to wane. Still, he was enjoying the hectic situation at the apartment. Last of the Conquerors now numbered 260,000 copies in print.[15] Smith began looking to other areas of writing—articles, short stories, and the like—and started moving in that direction, possibly because of the continual correspondence between his publishers and himself.

Whatever thoughts Smith may have entertained, he realized that the current novel he was working on needed completion. Farrar and Straus had already read the rough manuscript and had drawn up a contract for the book with the title "The Red Brick Castle."[16] Months later, not content with the title listed on the contract, Smith sent his editor a telegram saying, "[The] title should convey ironically idea of their [the plot characters'] sinfulness or play on transportation of the guilty and the innocent."[17] The same day he sent the telegram, he wrote his editor, Arthur Orrmont, a short note giving three titles that might be used: "The Sinners," "Tale of Two Sinners," and "The Poet and the Pickpocket."[18] Orrmont responded that "we are all enthused about [the title] 'Rowing in Eden,'" although that title was not the final one selected.[19] And while Mary was happy with her husband's completing his second book, other serious matters concerning their marriage remained below the surface.

In New York to visit his publisher's office, Smith, with his now "almost cocky, arrogant approach," spoke with Orrmont to sound out his opinion as to his writing ability.[20] Speaking frankly—Smith insisted on that—Orrmont explained, as carefully as he could, that Smith's style had more in common with "journalistic" writing than that of the novelist. He went on to say that in his opinion Smith would make a better journalist than a writer of fiction. Smith was crushed by Orrmont's candid, though requested, response, and he never spoke with his editor again.[21]

As with Last of the Conquerors, the title ultimately selected came from his editor, Orrmont. When the new novel was published in mid-1950, it bore the title Anger at Innocence.[22]

Smith's second novel, Anger at Innocence, is a study of good and evil as personified by the lead characters, Theodore Hall and Rodina Baleza. The story follows the ill-fated couple from their initial encounter and moves onward as their relationship develops. En route, several characters of meaningful consequence appear: Juarez, a jealous Mexican; Hucks, a truck driver; and Sylvia, Theodore's wife. Other characters of less importance appear, but are not completely realized.

The novel does not follow up on the successful theme of Last of the Conquerors. Moreover, Smith abandons any meaningful reference to Afro-Americans, although Juarez is singled out for his Mexican heritage. Anger at Innocence is a "white" story with slight racial protest. Protest is viewed, however, as Theodore's opposing Rodina's "evil" makeup and Rodina's attempts to impose her acquired "bad" values upon him, for she never totally succumbs to his "good" values for too long. The story is one of philosophic and psychological jockeying, using good versus evil as the goal.

Juarez appears early in the novel, and his character is probed as the story unfolds. Smith uses Juarez as a sort of prototype of the Black American male seeking to rise to the role of a man without racial stigma. Juarez attempts to deny his minority role and wants to assimilate into the American majority group in his pursuit of acceptance as a white male possibly to gain Rodina's acknowledgment of him as a suitor. The novel ends in violence as Smith composes an understated, yet complex story that employs existential undertones throughout. While the story lacks the use of Black characters, Juarez is generally treated as any darker-hued male in America. Anger at Innocence can best be described as Smith's "assimilationist" novel.[23]

The novel begins with Theodore Hall as he naps at his job as night watchman. He awakens and goes to a nearby diner for a snack. A noisy young couple causes him to think of his present age—thirty-nine—and to reflect on his wife of eighteen years and their not having any children. As he walks back to the plant, a young woman bumps into him and attempts to pick his wallet. He grabs her wrist and "whirl[s] to face her." The woman tries to escape, but he holds her tight. When he tells her he is going to call the police, she looks up at him; he discovers that she is a young girl, about "eighteen or nineteen." She stares at him but does not speak. Theodore has second thoughts about the police and releases her after securing a promise that she "won't steal anymore."

Sylvia, his wife, is introduced as "methodically" cleaning up their third-floor apartment in South Philadelphia. As Theodore arrives home, she asks him if he applied for a vacation and he tells her that he forgot. Their conversation is almost reduced to an argument and she says, "You'd probably have done much better, Theodore, marrying someone else." Casually she mentions that Howard, an earlier suitor, had visited her. "He asked about you," she tells him. "I should be suspicious," he laughs. "My former rival asking about me" (p. 14). Sylvia quietly thinks, "Former?" as Ted launches into his encounter with the young girl who tired to pick his pocket.

Anger at Innocence is melodramatic with too many coincidental events—such as the waiter's telling Ted "bad rain out tonight . . . nice night for pickpockets, huh?" (pp. 4-5)—that elicit disbelief and are too contirved. Theodore is also cast as a poet and intellectual; he is a do-gooder bogged down with a wife who considers him the "brave, shielding husband," on one hand, and yet a "coward" when he forgets to ask for a vacation at work.

Rodina Baleza is introduced as a young girl who moves "leisurely" on the empty streets late at night. She is described as having "a certain wildness." Subsequent to the incident with Theodore she returns to the ghetto of South Philadelphia. In an excited state resulting from her sudden capture by Ted, she nears the "four-story red brick house with the sagging front and the dirty windows and dirty steps" that is her home. Silently she enters her bedroom and goes to bed.

She awakens early the next morning in a room with twin beds. The other is occupied by her mother, who is an extremely cantankerous invalid. Her mother launches into bitter condemnation about her daughter's staying out late at night. Her mother continues as Rodina cleans the apartment and later decides to take a walk. About to leave the building, she hears a voice; the voice belongs to Hucks, a fellow tenant, who is described as having "the face of a man who looked like a prize fighter. . . . [He] was broad and blond and his face was square and thick; he might have been about twenty-five" (p. 23). They had, at one time, been more than friends. He is on his way to work as a truck driver and reminds her to their past status.

She enters a restaurant adjacent to the tenement. As she is having coffee, Juarez appears in the doorway. He is "a scrawny man, with dark skin, thick features, and shiny straight black hair" (pp. 24-25). She asks him to join her. Their conversation concerns her pickpocket role; he thinks she will wind up in jail. Later that night she walks on the street where the night before she had attempted to pick Ted's wallet. She notices a lighted window, looks in, and sees Ted. She knocks on the window, and he opens the door. They talk briefly about the previous night's encounter and then go to the diner to talk further. She wants to know if he is married. "Yes," he says, adding that he does not have any children. She is impressed by his demeanor. As he returns to work, he asks her: "Will you come again sometime?" (p. 31). She agrees.

Rodina returns to see Theodore often at the plant. He never attempts to make a pass at her—she is amazed!—and "he is not like the men she knew. . . . Somehow, because she knew him, she, too, felt decent" (p. 35). She feels there is "nothing wrong in stealing" and had been doing it since "she was a little girl." One morning as he is about to leave work, she appears. He walks her home. She remains silent until they reach the front of the red brick tenement where she lives. She tells him: "This is home. When we first came here I loved this place. I used to pretend it was a castle and tell myself that someday my king would come to live here with me."[24] She enters the building, and Ted goes home.

The months later Theodore finds his life changing due to his attraction to Rodina. He visits her mother. Mrs. Baleza is anxious to meet him; her daughter has not told her he is married. She tells him, "I wasn't too sure of Rodina's choices. She's picked up so many tramps." They chat as Rodina sits quietly nearby. Abruptly, Mrs. Baleza says her daughter "always will be evil, and her evil will spread to any man who fools with her. Mark my word" (p. 42). Theodore and Rodina are embarrassed; as they leave he tells her, she has "got to get away from this." He asks her if she loves him; Rodina agrees that she does.

Next morning Sylvia and Ted go for a walk in the nearby park, where she tries to engage him in small talk. He tells her, "I hate to say this. I don't quite know how to explain it. . . . I want a divorce." She is stunned and stares at him. They return to the apartment, where she, surprisingly, helps him pack a suitcase. He leaves.

William Gardner Smith, within the first four chapters, has

introduced the novel's major characters and the separation of the Halls. Ted now moves to the tenement where Rodina lives and secures a room "formerly occupied by a gangster, now safely tucked away in jail." The location now becomes the pivotal locale for the balance of the book.

As Ted gets settled in his room, he finds some articles left by the previous tenant, including a loaded gun. He replaces the gun in "the drawer . . . . and closed it." Ted feels happy and tells Rodina: "You'll make a wonderful wife." Rodina: "Wife?" "Yes," he says, "wife." Later that night he asks her to sleep with him. He notices her embarrassment as she agrees. He says, "I don't want to touch you. I just want you to sleep beside me" (p. 54). Smith at this point is befuddling; one senses that Theodore's character has not been fully examined for such a statement to seem realistic or that Smith is assuming too much of the reader. Even stranger, Rodina renders approval of the situation.

The next morning, Juarez, in his room, looks out the window at Rodina and Ted on the street below, thinking about them. He remembers how "she used to come to him for advice and comfort." He broods about Hucks's "bigness" and his "bully" attitude and decides that he and Rodina have that much in common. He goes to work; when he finishes his job, he meets Juanita, a Mexican girl who loves him. They attend a movie, then visit her cousin. Later, he takes her home, where she tells him he is a wonderful person and that she loves him. He questions why she loves him and then decides to end their relationship.

Meanwhile, Theodore's position at the plant is terminated when the manager finds out he has left his wife. He tells Rodina about his being fired; she responds, "I always bring trouble." She returns to picking pockets and is unfortunate enough to pick a plainclothes policeman's wallet; he attempts to arrest her, but she runs off with his wallet. She gets to the safety of the hallway of the tenement, where she encounters Hucks; he knows what has just happened. She offers him the contents of the wallet, but he asks her to go to his room. "Go to hell!" she says. But the threat Hucks poses—telling Theodore—is real; her hatred of him is not as great as the fear of Theodore's finding out about the pickpocket episode. "Theodore <u>must not</u> find out" is the rationale she uses for agreeing to go Hucks's room. As they enter his room, they are noticed by Juarez.

Theodore finds a job as a salesman at a "photographic supplies store"—as Smith also did—and is unaware of Rodina and Hucks's clandestine meeting. She begins to wonder if she should tell him about Hucks; maybe that would get him to to back to Sylvia. With mixed emotions, she goes to the tearoom and talks with Juarez.

In his own way Juarez loves Rodina, knowing full well she would never have him as a suitor. His hatred for Hucks is now unbearable, so he devises a plan that will alter any chance of Hucks's bothering Rodina again: Since she is hopelessly "evil" and Ted "good," why not get Ted to change, to become "evil" for the "good" of both? Rodina listens to his plan, but does not want that; she wants Theodore to remain good. Theodore, meanwhile, has sensed that something is troubling Rodina. He wonders if it could be the delay in getting his divorce or something from her past, possibly a "former lover now molesting her again." His thoughts are interrupted as the landlady, Mrs. Houston, invites him and Rodina to a party in her apartment. He agrees to attend.

Fifteen people, fellow tenants, are milling about when Rodina and Ted enter. Hucks is there; still longing for Rodina, he thinks that through insulting Ted or challenging his manhood he can win her back. Juarez sits quietly witnessing the participants. Theodore attempts to fight Hucks, but is shoved across the room as Rodina joins in the fracas. The scene closes with Ted and Rodina going to his room, where he "listen[s] to the epithets pouring endlessly from Rodina" (p. 177).

By February they are sleeping together—"without clothes"—and Rodina is deeply in love with Theodore. On one occasion she leaves the room and has a few drinks at the nearby bar, then returns to the room. They get in bed and, "letting passion flow unrestrained," make love. The following night a joyful Theodore and happy Rodina meet Juarez sitting in the tearoom. Hucks enters the building, and Juarez calls him to join them. The tormented lovers remain silent in Hucks's presence. Juarez wants to seize the opportunity of Theodore, Rodina, and Hucks's being together to bait the three into taking positions or exposing recent wounds, but Rodina and Ted leave.

Rodina tells Theodore that her mother needs an operation that will cost a sizeable amount. She knows they do not have the money and volunteers to return to picking pockets for the cost of medical bill. He is shocked and, to get the money, steals two cameras from his job. He gives her the cameras and assumes she will sell the stolen items to defray the cost of the operation. His guilt at stealing the cameras brings his "good" into play: He quits the job rather than see an innocent stock boy discharged. When he tells Rodina about his resignation at the store, she realizes her plan has backfired; he is still a "good" man, because stealing the cameras was negated by his voluntary resignation. She is now caught up with her own thoughts and, feeling guilty, questions him about Sylvia. The landlady appears and informs Rodina that her mother is very sick. She rushes to her mother's room as Ted goes to the tearoom, where he is met by Juarez. Juarez asks about Rodina, and Ted tells him about her mother's sickness brought on since her operation. Juarez tells him she "had no operation" (p. 235). Meanwhile, Rodina discovers her mother has actually died. She is buried two days later. Rodina goes to Theodore's room and asks him, "as though from a great distance . . . 'Ted, would you kill someone for me?'" He thinks she is upset by her mother's death, but tells her he would not. She assures him she would kill for him and remains in a "far away" state. Theodore thinks to himself about the number of recent important occurrences: What do they mean? Sensing that she has recovered sufficiently, he asks her about her mother's operation. Rodina assures him she always tells the truth.

Smith tediously moves the novel toward its conclusion with several unresolved situations still to be settled. The main characters move sharply into each others' paths as the pace of Anger at Innocence increases.

Juarez prods Theodore as they sit in the tearoom, playing "subtly upon his dislike and fear of Hucks." Ted wants to know Juarez' interest in the matter, thus forcing Juarez' response: "I am simply interested in people. I am fascinated by emotions." Later, Juarez meets Hucks and wants to talk about Rodina; he tells a startled Hucks, "She loves you Hucks; she can't help herself. She even told me she's been to bed with you since [Theodore] came here to live, and how much she enjoyed it" (p. 253). Hucks consciously takes the bait and later, when he sees Rodina, attempts to strike up a conversation with her, but she does not respond. Lusting for her, he seizes and kisses her. She calls for Ted, who comes rushing to her defense with a lamp, striking it against Hucks's head. The blow staggers him as Rodina cries: "Kill him, Ted! Kill him, Ted! Kill him!" (p. 270). Hucks recognizes from the harshness of her voice that she really wants him dead. They stand looking at each other until Hucks leaves.

Theodore, in deep thought, remembers the urgency in her voice as she told him to kill Hucks: Why did she hate Hucks? Finally, he asks her if Hucks "used to be your boy friend." She agrees that he was, although she now hates Hucks. Silent, Ted is not satisfied. He later notices the landlady cleaning up the late Mrs. Baleza's room for a new boarder. She suggests that he take few of Rodina's items to her. As he opens a drawer, he looks at the two stolen cameras he thought Rodina had sold; now he understands what has been going on and his thoughts of Rodina are clearer.

As Ted prepares to visit Sylvia, Rodina arrives. He does not tell her about the cameras or his other thoughts. He leaves for his wife's apartment. Rodina subsequently goes to the tearoom for a few drinks, spots Hucks, and invites him to join her. He sits down, trying to understand her change in attitude. She asks him, "How am I in bed?" and offers to go to bed with him. Theodore, meanwhile, discovers that there is no response to his knock at Sylvia's door. He returns to the tenement and finds Rodina out. Juarez opens the door, and Ted asks him if he has seen Rodina. "Juarez stare[s] at him . . . his eyes [are] filled with bitterness. 'Yes,' he answer[s] . . . 'Where she always is when you're not home. In bed. With Hucks'" (p. 295). Ted controls his temper until Juarez leaves.

Ted begins packing his clothes and goes to the bureau to get his shirts. He notices the forgotten gun and thinks about committing suicide. Rodina enters the room and looks at the suitcase. A growing hysteria embraces her. She looks at the gun as Theodore asks her: "Where have you been . . . or will you lie to me again?" He is angry as she tells him,

> "Downstairs, with Hucks, in bed with Hucks."
> His eyes fell. Her heart sank. "Downstairs in bed with Hucks," she repeated. He breathed heavily, but did

> not move. "Shoot! Shoot!" she cried.
>
> He looked up at her in surprise. Shoot? He was conscious of the gun in his hand, and surprise turned to something near amusement. Shoot? . . .
>
> "Coward! . . ." she screamed, "Coward! . . . Shoot!"

William Gardner Smith concludes the tortured relationship with an unexpected turn.

> But he only smiled, looked at the gun, and then tossed it to the bed.
>
> With a cry of despair she sprang upon the gun: tears flushed from her eyes. Screaming soundlessly, she pointed the gun at him and pulled the trigger twice.
>
> With great surprise, he felt the bullets strike into his chest. Slowly, not comprehending, he fell to the floor. Swiftly life flowed from the wounds, like water from a basin when the stopper is removed. He closed his eyes, not knowing. The last sounds he heard were a faint sobbing cry, and then the roar of another shot, seeming to come from a great distance, mingling with the clamor of a street car passing by (pp. 297-98).

After the deaths of Theodore and Rodina, Smith anticlimactically returns the story to Sylvia, who is "trying on the new hat." She thinks almost sadistically about Theodore, not knowing about his death, sure that "he would not visit her. He could not bear facing her again." She looks at the clock anticipating Howard's arrival. In this flashback Smith, it appears, has underscored the scene of Theodore's knocking at his wife's door and not getting a response. He intimates either that Sylvia and Howard were out or symbolically using the new hat she is trying on, that maybe she and Howard were at the apartment, involved, when Ted arrived unexpectedly.

The novel finally ends on still another tragic note. The night after the deaths of Theodore and Rodina, the landlady opens Juarez's door:

> The room was dark. Mrs. Davis called, and got no answer, and tried the light switch, which did not work. She was conscious, first of all, of the odor of the room: dank, musty, like old unused books, with the faint clinging of stale cigarette smoke. Then gradually there came to her senses the sounds: the faint falling of rain on the window panes intermingled with the hiss of wind through trees, green now but not yet mature in the adolescent Spring. Only after these things had come to the old, slow, wheezing woman who had cried all night because of the tragedy, did she notice, against the faint glow of the window, the dim outline of the body, brown and thin and stooped, swinging like a boxer's sandbag or a football team's dummy from the rope tied to the rickety old chandelier (p. 300).

Anger at Innocence was Smith's only attempt at writing a novel without Afro-American characters. In writing about non-Black people, ironically, his characters seem to talk in almost rhythmic Black language, using slum venacular of the late 1940s. The basic fault of the novel is that it is laden with excess writing that could have been shortened by eliminating some of the detailed landscape of South Philadelphia. Excesses also occur in needless dialogue and contrived events just prior to a happening. Nevertheless, the novel is interesting because it shows the range of interests that Smith possesses. The book also shows Smith's attraction to violence, as in the *Last of the Conquerors*; Rodina's killing Theodore is another example of the lovestruck German girl who kills her soldier-lover in that novel. *Anger at Innocence* does not have the strength of the previous book; that is, Smith is not writing about a subject or a lifestyle he is familiar with. Critical reviews of the novel were mixed. Carl Milton Hughes in study *The Negro Novelist*, commented: "The novel exhibits competent writing. . . . The author weakens his drama with improbabilities. . . . Smith rules out a great deal of human qualities in the two [leading] characters. . . . The novel, therefore, is only partially successful."[25] Alain Locke, writing criticism about literature of the Negro for 1950 stated that *Anger at Innocence* "is largely journeyman reporting, with all the faults of melodramas, superficial stock characterization, banality and cliche situation. The drama unrolls in tabloid newspaper fashion, with little to commend it to serious readers."[26] Author Robert Kingery, describing the novel in the *Library Journal*, said, "Violent, brutal in incident and language, this book seems to be (in spite of much bitterness), a serious attempt to examine the nature of good and evil through a number of characters clearly and realistically drawn. As such it is recommended for collections aiming to include contemporary fiction of literary merit."[27]

On the Way to Paris 3

The "literary and political salon," as the West Philadelphia apartment of the Smiths was called, became a meeting spot for a cross-section of people with Communist, Socialist, and Trotskyite postures.[1] Liberals, Democrats, Republicans, both Black and white, appeared to be vying for William Gardner Smith's attention. While he enjoyed the excitement, Mary now accepted the sometimes "circus atmosphere," as was later said, with reservations. Her background and training would not have allowed for a number of situations that, by now, were to be expected. Heated debates, outright arguments, the "selling" of one's philosophic position—all made for a lively discussion whenever guests arrived.

Among the guests, Richard Gibson was an almost constant fixture. Although he was attending Kenyon College in Gambier, Ohio, during the school year, on his return to Philadelphia, other than being at his grandmother's home, he was to be found mostly at the apartment of Bill and Mary Smith. He and Smith continued their ongoing discussions of writing, authors, the arts, and a range of topics that had begun at Smith's South 20th Street residence. One guest, rightly or wrongly, noted in Gibson "that his manner [was] (snifty), his speech, (glib, rapid-fire, seemingly all-knowing) and his actions those of an agent provocateur."[2]

Gibson was an extremely articulate young man and was always in the company of the "right" people; one saw in him non-Black qualities, usually understood in the ghetto as emulating "the man." His persuasive attitude was responsible, in part, for securing a trip to Yaddo, the artists and writers' colony at Saratoga Springs, New York. Through the sponsorship of a white patron and liberal, Mrs. Irene Rose, Gibson was accepted for a month's stay at Yaddo in May 1951. He probably spoke to Mrs. Rose about Smith's also attending Yaddo, as Bill was accepted for a stay there a month later. It appears, however, Smith spent his time there thinking deeply about his situation in Philadelphia, focusing particularly on Mary and their relationship.[3] How could he have known the Federal Bureau of Investigation was developing a file on him and had already labled him a Communist.[4]

Yaddo was probably the best thing that could have happened to Smith. He was off by himself and could think current problems out clearly and objectively. It appears that among the varied thoughts he had was to leave America for a period of time, possibly a year. At the Yaddo retreat he probably spoke with others about their travels abroad. Eventually he made plans to go to Paris by the autumn of 1951. Once he mentioned the proposed trip to Mary, she joined in the excitement. Passports were needed, and a travel agency was to be contacted. Accomodations were secured for the trip; they would sail from New York on October 13 aboard the French liner Liberté, to arrive at Le Havre, France, on October 19. Six days after applying for passports, they were issued on September 27.[5]

The frantic pace of getting what seemed a million things settled in Philadelphia finally ended on October 12. They caught a New York-bound train in the afternoon, checked into Hotel Roosevelt, then went to dinner. Smith had an appointment with Carl Van Vechten to sit for several photographs for the latter's collection of famous Negroes.[6]

Early the following morning they left the hotel to board the ship. A pleasant surprise awaited them. As Smith described it in a letter to his mother: "It was a wonderful surprise to find you and Edna and Lucy [his aunts] had come to see us off. Things like that make me realize all the more how lucky I am to have such people care about me."[7] The Liberté left the berth at noontime. In a short span of time the New York harbor and skyline grew small, then smaller, then disappeared.

Almost immediately they began meeting other passengers. Writing home while still aboard ship, Smith said, "The people are really lovely; some of them we'll visit in Paris, others in England. The people are from many countries, and most can't speak English to well. However, we manage to communicate."[8] Bill and Mary took the sometimes rough weather and rolling sea in stride. Most evenings Smith was to be found in the ship's ballroom awaiting the nightly dance to begin.[9] In describing his activities and attitude aboard the ship, a fellow passenger remembered that she had "met Bill . . . and had a wonderful time dancing with him as we both loved to dance. I found him likeable, charming, life-loving, brash. He was spreading his wings, eager for every kind of experience and tremendously interested in everything." Moreover, she reflected on the fact that "he was . . . very young, particularly young to have the kind of success he quickly found, and as result, very cocky—a trait which, given the circumstances and his charm, was not unsympathetic."[10]

The six-day Atlantic crossing terminated on the morning of October 19 with the Smiths bidding farewells to newfound acquaintances. Family, friends, Philadelphia, America, the Atlantic Ocean were now behind them. Ironically, the hotel they checked into, Hôtel des Etats-Unis, meant Hotel of the United

States.

Six months before Last of the Conquerors was published, an article by Black journalist Roi Ottley, called "Black Frenchmen," had appeared in Negro Digest. It began, simply enough by stating: "French liberalism towards races and colors is no myth. The equality and fraternity and liberty inscribed upon the public buildings in France since the Revolution, are realities in so far as social intercourse is concerned. Nor is there condenscension in this. . . . To an extent equalled by few cities in the world, Paris is the nearest approach to civilized living for the black man. He unquestionably has personal diginity, freedom of movement, may work at any occupation he is qualified to do."[11] The article continued, in part to say,

> Andre Gide once said: "The less intelligent the white man is, the more stupid the black man seems to him."
>
> Paris has a black population of roughly twenty thousand, mainly from Africa, the West Indies and the United States. . . . There is, of course, no "Negro neighbornood" in Paris. Nor are there such places as "Negro" cafes, restaurants, barber shops, cabaret, beauty salons or hotels, though there are Negro owners of such places.[12]

Ottley went on to give examples of the total "assimilative powers" France allegedly possessed. The article ended: "Beyond employment at any rate, the black Frenchman has few tangible grievances as a race in France. What legitimate grievances he does have are those common to workmen and the poor. But a period of prosperity in France would overcome this one obstacle to his total integration."[13]

While the figure of twenty thousand for the Black population appears to be rather high for the year 1948, Richard Wright, writing about the American Negro's status in France three years and a half after the Ottley article and a few months before Smith left America, remarked:

> Because there are no Black belts in France which would enable heads to be counted in a racial manner, there are no official figures on the number of American Negroes in the French community. Rough estimates claim that there are more than 500 American Negroes in France, about half of which reside permanently or temporarily in Paris, the rest being scattered throughout the provinces. Occupationally, they comprise a diverse and varied lot, ranging from GI students, journalists, doctors, governmental employees, musicians, entertainers, independent artists, and writers who are self-supporting and make their contribution to the daily life of France.[14]

Such was the atmosphere Smith would find. He had had an illustrious predecessor in France.

Richard Wright and his family had visited France from May 1946 until almost mid-January 1947, when they returned to New York.[15] Wright's return brought him face to face again with his lifelong enemy: racism.[16] Rather than be attacked by "young white hoodlums," Wright, being "afraid for his family," began making plans to return to a place of freedom from insults and possible physical violence.[17] At the end of July 1947, the Wrights left America for Paris; the departure would signal Richard Wright's beginning his exile and expatriation from his native soil.[18]

During the time the Smiths were planning to go to Paris, as well as at the time of their arrival, the picture of events painted by Wright were actually accurate. The Wright article continued stating:

> But something has begun to happen to the U.S. Negro in France; a new kind of anxiety has entered his consciousness; and this new worry has nothing to do with Frenchmen or their behavior towards him. With the advent of the Marshall Plan and the Atlantic Pact, the U.S. Negro has witnessed the spread and deepening of American influence in France. The constricting racial influences from which he had fled seems to be coming nearer to him across the Atlantic. For the first time since he landed in France as a refugee visitor, the U.S. Negro is asking himself: To what extent will some Frenchmen, eager to please Americans, accept racial doctrines alien to French traditions or customs?
>
> Our quarrel, frankly, as U.S. Negroes, is with our fellow countrymen, those white Americans who take pride in damning French life and culture 24 hours a day; white Americans, who, while speaking out of one side of their mouths about freedom and democracy, continue to practice racial exclusiveness.[19]

This might or may not have been known—probably not—to Mary and Bill Smith as they packed for the trip and embarked for France. They were now, however, in the midst of the City of Light.

On Friday, October 19, the train from Le Havre arrived in Paris on time. It was a pleasant ride with excitement running high for Mary and Bill. As the train rolled to a stop at Gare Saint-Lazare, a familiar face came to view; Harry Goldberg, whom Smith had met earlier in the year in Philadelphia and who was in Paris attending the Sorbonne as a transfer student, completing his Master's degree requirements in library science, loomed smilingly before them.[20] After helping Bill and Mary get settled in the hotel, he proceeded to show them the sights. Goldberg would act as a guide for the immediate future, immensely enjoying the company of these fellow Philadelphians.

Once comfortably in place at the hotel, where they stayed several weeks, Smith reviewed some of the items he had to complete. Among them, he had to meet his Paris agent. He wrote home,

> I went to see my Paris agent yesterday. She's a woman about 50, and lives in a fabulous apartment; she's very famous here. I also met the man . . . who translated my second book into French. It will be brought out next February, and will also be brought out by the book club here, which is very big. Next week, I will be interviewed by one of the big magazines here, and I am being accepted into membership by a big book society.[21]

The letter, written to his mother within two weeks of his arrival continued,

> Although we are at present living in one room (a lovely room) of a hotel (at approximately $1.60 per night), we feel that we have an extra room in the big coffee house down the street. . . . I go to the coffee house in the morning and carry a stack of paper with me; then I sit for a couple of hours over a cup of coffee, writing notes for the novel I am going to work on over here. . . . The people who own the coffee houses want you to consider their place your home; and we do![22]

Living in a standard hotel room was not what either desired; they needed an apartment, a "real" place where "Mary [can] do the cooking for us."[23] Smith explained how they found their apartment:

> The apartment is on another floor of the hotel, and we were very luck to get it. The hotel manager took a liking to us, I think, and one day asked me if I'd like an apartment. It will cost about $55 a month, but you can't do any better in Paris right now; the price includes heat, gas, electricity, and maid service to change our linen and towels and make our bed and clean up in general. The apartment consists of one large room, plus a small bedroom and a small kitchen. We'll do something with it.
>
> The problem of money is not bothering us yet, but it will in a few months. At present, Mary and I have to eat in restaurants, which charge about 75 cents apiece for sumptuous meals. . . . Food and board are the main financial drains at present (not to mention amusement), but even these two things will sap our small reserves in about three months, so I've got my fingers crossed about the possibility of selling some fiction. Anyway, I'm not worried; I don't worry much . . . (maybe I don't worry enough!).[24]

Interestingly enough, he mentions in one sentence, "I met Richard Wright, and spent an evening in his home; he's very nice, just an ordinary Joe, and has two lovely children."[25]

Shortly before Christmas, two months after their arrival, he described his observations, what Mary and himself were doing, and his thoughts about the holiday season:

> It's nice to think of you at Christmas; I think that time, more than any other, is a symbol of the closeness we feel to each other. We—our family—always had the most beautiful Christmases I ever saw anywhere. I remember the fun (from years back) of decorating the tree; I remember the greatest fun of all—that of exchanging presents (which we'd bought with money saved with difficulty—remember?); and I remember my own pleasure, in the days before Christmas, in reading newspapers with the kids, looking at things which were for sail [sic], making them more and more excited about the approach of Christmas—and then, going downstairs with them, the shining balls, the presents. Makes me feel old and wise!—just think, I watched at their first Christmas; and I participated, each year, in their excitement. I feel extremely close to them; someday, perhaps, they'll know it.
>
> Christmas here is very different from the Christmases in the States. If you didn't look at the calender [sic] you might not realize that it was approaching Christmas at all—for the French celebrate the day only as a day for giving small gifts to children. They don't make a big fuss about it like we do. I prefer our way.
>
> This is the second Christmas I spend in a strange, European city—and, funny to say, I don't feel like a stranger at all. I feel at home in Paris.[26]

He went on to say,

> I like the people I've been meeting. Canada Lee was here for two weeks, and practically lived in our apartment. (I was even working to find a girlfriend for him while he was here!) Then, too, we are friends of the Richard Wright's, and see him fairly frequently. (We've eaten at his house.)
>
> I'm working hard on a new book, which I think is good. I've also agreed to do a weekly column from Europe for the Pittsburgh Courier, in order to make extra some money (I'd be over here starving otherwise!) They'll pay a hundred bucks a month for the column—not bad.
>
> I forgot to tell you about my literary life. As you know, my second book is being brought out here . . . by both a publisher and a book club—so both, naturally, are happy that I am here, for publicity reasons. . . . But the real life—my life, at the present time—is in my own quarter (a section, like South Philly), which happens to be one of the nicest in Paris.
>
> When I write next, I'll tell you about some of the places we've visited—not the "tourist attractions," which I don't care much for (and leave for Mary to

visit), but the smaller, nicer, real Parisian places.[27]

Unbeknownst to Smith, less than two weeks earlier the Department of State alerted "certain American Diplomatic and Consular Officers" that

> The Department desires to receive any information which may come to your attention regarding the activities of William Gardner Smith. . . .
>
> Smith has been actively associated with the Philadelphia branch of the Socialist Workers Party and has been active in both the Philadelphia chapter of the Civil Rights Congress and the Philadelphia Council of the Arts, Sciences, and Professions.[28]

Smith, in the meantime, had completed and forwarded his first article from Paris to the Pittsburgh Courier; it dealt with how "the life of Paris is in the cafes" under the heading "European Backdrop."[29]

The lack of money was slowly ebbing their spirits. Something had to give, but what? The spoke about it almost daily. Abruptly, a solution was reached: Mary would go to England and try to secure employment; Smith would remain in Paris and continue writing. The loosely structured plan was not what he really wanted; actually he wanted Mary to return to Philadelphia to a life, level, and place she knew. And, while Mary could obviously see what her husband was implying, her position was to stay near, as near as possible, to him, even if it meant the natural boundary of the English channel.

In early January 1952, less than three months after their arrival in Paris, Mary left for England. She took up residence in Sussex Gardens where, daily, she tried to secure employment. The race problem was moving into its earliest stages—discrimination—in postwar England, and she could not get a position, although she continued searching for two months. Realizing that her meager funds were rapidly running out and that she might, indeed, not find any suitable work, she contacted her father in Philadelphia, requesting funds for return passage. The money was duly forwarded, but she gambled that maybe, if she remained just a little longer, a job would materialize. The venture did not pay off. Again her father sent money; and again she gambled and lost. On her third request for money, her father stated he would send no more, and this time she decided to return to Philadelphia.

Meanwhile, in Paris, Smith continued writing and wondered how everything would work out. He was not going to return to America at this time; he loved Paris and was convinced that he would make it in some manner. He remained at the Hôtel de Tournon, visiting the cafe across the street almost daily to make notes for the new novel and to meet the clientele of his "extended" apartment. He constantly thought of Mary, of her being near and yet so far away in England. His thoughts were filled with many things, one of which were the financial difficulties that were bombarding Mary and himself. Something had to be done; a decision had to be reached immediately. Finally in mid-March 1952 he wrote his mother:

> This letter must begin by letting you know about something very important and, for me, very sad. Mary and I are, at least temporarily, separated. For the past two months, she has been living in London. I returned to Paris Saturday [March 8], after having visited her for two weeks in London—to say goodbye. She is, this minute, on board a ship bound for home. . . .
>
> The separation is no sudden thing. The things which led to it began, both Mary and I knew, almost from the first day that we were married. I should say, first of all that I love, respect, and regard Mary as highly today as I did the day we were married; and she feels the same way about me. The fact is, however, that marriage, to her, is not for me; and marriage, to me, should not be for her. We are too utterly different in every conceivable way.
>
> I am not a builder. She is. I am absolutely unhappy paying a mortgage, paying an insurance policy, buying furniture, having friends in politely for the evening, having a beautiful apartment, etc. I cannot stand that confinement and that safety. I cannot write in that homey atmosphere! Mary needs a home. She needs comforts, affection, to be near her parents, to be settled and steady. I go absolutely crazy in the same situation. I can't stand to be settled for life. I want to move. I want always to live, to discover something new. The boredom of marriage drove me nearly crazy.
>
> I can't explain myself. I know I am different from most other people, in that the things which are important to them are not important to me, and vice versa. . . . Two months ago, since Mary was in England, I found myself with only thirty francs—ten cents—in my pocket. I was reduced, for a period of about three weeks, to eating only one full meal a day, which I cooked myself, on a single alcohol burner, in my small hotel room. For the rest, I ate cheese and bread. I was forced then, and still do, to wash all my own clothes, iron, etc. I lived, for awhile, only by borrowing. I lost ten pounds—which, for me, is a lot. And yet I was happy! Because I was living the way I want to live. I cannot, however, ask a wife as delicate and sweet as Mary to live such a life with me.
>
> The Christmas of 1950 . . . I told Mary I wanted our marriage to come to an end. That was after only one year of marriage. She was thunderstruck. We talked it over. We decided to try again. It was no good. When I went to YADDO, last summer, it was only to get away for awhile, to think. When I came back, and we decided to come to Europe, it was because we knew that if we stayed in Philly our marriage was doomed, and we thought that we

> might be able to save it by coming here, seeing new things, starting new. That didn't help either. So we've done what we've done.
>
> I know that this letter must come as a shock. I'm truly sorry, but we did not act hastily, and still agree—both of us—that it was the only way. There's no talk of divorce yet. Mary will wait as long as she likes—then make up her mind what she wants to do: stay married, and hope I'll change (which I won't), or go ahead with a divorce.[30]

With Mary returning to Philadelphia, Smith could now pursue his life, writing, and whatever lay in the immediate future with clearer thoughts and with a new excitement: his personal freedom to explore *anything* to his heart's delight. He was now on his own, far, far, from Philadelphia, his immediate family, and Mary. William Gardner Smith was now twenty-five years old.

Spring was underway several weeks when Smith was notified famed actor Canada Lee had died on May 9. Lee, who had completed the motion picture *Cry, the Beloved Country* in South Africa, had visited him and Mary in their Paris apartment. It was there they noticed Lee did not look well; he himself complained of being tired. The two weeks Lee spent during December in their company would be the last time they would see him. Smith wrote about him in a newspaper article in late May titled "Friend Reveals Hate Hurt Canada [Lee] Deeply" and quoted Lee in a letter sent him from New York: "I got here to find myself on the . . . blacklist. I don't know why. Anyway, it's impossible to find a job."[31]

During the autumn of 1952 Smith began what can best be described as numerous liaisons in Europe. He met a young Canadian woman; they lived together sharing views, meals, and bed.[32] This encounter marked the first of a series of women he would meet over an extended period in Paris. Meantime, Smith continued writing and taking notes while having coffee at the Café le Tournon. His chance meetings with other writers, poets, artists, and an assortment of nonartistic types continued. Among the people he met or would meet were James Baldwin, Joke Beretti, Heather Chisholm, Beauford Delaney, Dean Dixon, Gait Froge, Katia Grotkamp, Ollie Harrington, Leroy Haynes, Gordon Heath, Chester Himes, Christopher Logue, Pamela Oline, Larry Potter, Bernard Redmont, Christopher Scott, Art Simmons, John Singleton, and Layna Verin.

Smith managed to keep his name in print partially by writing articles for *Ebony* magazine. One ariticle was the "The Oldest Negro in Paris"[33]; another was "Black Boy in Paris," concerning Richard Wright.[34] During this period Wright said to Smith, "Writing . . . would always be a way of thinking aloud over issues—posing the problems and the questions as to their solutions—posing them only, not answering them."[35] This statement by Wright, considered the dean of Afro-American writers in Paris, would be an almost subliminal guide to Smith's future writing.[36] And although keeping his name in print was one of the reasons for the *Ebony* articles, the money problem was a constant threat. In a letter to his mother he said, "I am the Paris correspondent for JET and EBONY magazines; JET pays me $25 per week, and EBONY pays for the stories I do for them from time to time."[37]

But he was constantly without funds and borrowed money from Harry Goldberg, his fellow Philadelphian, who was having a hard time living on his GI educational benefits.[38] Smith continued in his letter:

> This summer, I expect to go down to Rome, Italy, for a month or so. . . . The life here is . . . for me, very rich . . . from the point of view of my personal "education," this trip has been marvelous. No matter what happens afterwards, I'll always have this.
>
> One of my friends is Ollie Harrington, who draws "Dark Laughter" (Bootsie) cartoons in the Pittsburgh Courier. By the way, did I tell you that, when my column stopped in the Courier, the paper got so many letters that they wrote and asked me to come back to them? I refused, because JET had already offered me a job, and I knew that I would work for JET and EBONY whenever I return to the United States. All the same, I felt good that public pressure forced The Courier to ask me back.[39]

Chester Himes, who arrived in Paris during the early spring of 1953 and met Smith through Richard Wright, recalls:

> One day Dick [Wright] asked me if I knew William Gardner Smith . . . and I said I would like to meet him. Dick took me over to the Café Tournon . . . and introduced me to a moderately tall, pleasant looking brownskinned young man who talked very rapidly in choppy, broken sentences, and said how glad he was to meet me, but it was very obvious that he and Dick did not like each other at all. The *Last of the Conquerors* had not been published in France . . . but Bill had written another book . . . *Anger at Innocence*, which had been selected by a book club in France, and since none of Dick's books had ever received that doubtful distinction, I think Bill felt a little superior about the matter, which was very normal for one so young, and he was young. Youth was the most outstanding characteristic of William Gardner Smith—youth and naivete.[40]

A couple of months later, during July, Himes remembers:

> I ran into . . . Smith and a fat sleepy-looking girl in the Café Suisse . . . whom he introduced as Heather Chisholm, from Canada. When I introduced him to Alva, Bill gave her a glance and said, "Oh, there are lots of white American women around the Latin Quarter." Alva startled us all with one of her outbursts of laughter.

Bill said I'd written the book If He Hollers Let Him Go and Heather said, "Eenie, meenie, minie, moe—" and Bill interrupted, jokingly perhaps, "Don't you say it!"[41]

Smith's life in Paris had, by now, reached a point at which his daily activities fell into a routine:

> My day goes like this. I get up about 10:30 or 11:00 in the morning, make some coffee, and immediately go to work. (I should describe, first of all, my room: rather [small], with a double bed, two closets, a wash bowl, a bookcase, a bedtable and a table on which I work. The window looks out onto a small, lively Paris street, and now, as I write, I hear voices, the honking of horns, the roar of traffic. On the wall of the room are some reproductions of famous paintings, and also a big, clear map of Paris. On top of the bookcase is a dish which I keep always filled with fruit. Also, I keep in the room a small alcohol burner—something you can't get in the States—on which I heat water for coffee, etc.) By "go to work" I mean that I stick some paper into the typewriter and sit down in front of it. I eat some fruit, while sitting there, and, if still hungry, call downstairs and order some breakfast sent up to me—a kind of French rolls, butter and coffee. Anyway, I work until lunchtime—about 2:00 or 3:00—then go down the street to a little restaurant where you can get a meal, including soup first and dessert afterwards, for 75 cents. (Food is about the only thing which is relatively cheap in Paris; clothes are outrageously expensive.) After the meal, I go across the street to my favorite little cafe.
>
> This cafe is called the Café de Tournon. It's small, not immaculately clean, and kind of noisy. Every day some Frenchmen, old and young, sit around there playing cards, checkers or chess. They also try to get me to play bridge, but I refuse, though I've learned how to play. I don't like that game very much. . . . Around 4:30 or 5:00 I return to my room and work until 7:00 and am free for the evening. Sometimes I visit friends. Sometimes I go back to the Café de Tournon, or go to other cafes. Sometimes I take in movies, concerts, etc. And sometimes, though rarely, I return to my room to read.[42]

Smith, who needed funds most of the time after Mary's return to the States, was always borrowing small amounts of money to tide him over. The subtle approach for a loan from Himes went like this:

> One night at the Café Tournon, in his abrupt jerky way, Bill Smith asked me if I wanted to take a walk down to the Seine with him. I said all right. . . .
>
> All Bill wanted was to borrow twenty-five hundred francs to go to Ringside, the jazz joint. . . . I went

along with Bill, but nothing interesting happened.[43]

Meanwhile, in late September, Smith's passport was renewed for two years.[44]

The novel Smith had been working on was now finished. He had selected the title this time, and the book would be dedicated to Mary, now living in Philadelphia. Commenting on the story he said, "This book . . . will be the best thing yet, I think. It's called "South Street," and is, naturally about that Street in the main. Places like the Postal Card and Showboat [two night clubs in Philadelphia] come into the story. The book has a lot of characters, including a numbers writer and a committeeman (also a Blues singer)."[45] In 1954 Smith's third novel, South Street, was published.[46]

Willian Gardner Smith returns to the South Philadelphia scene with his novel, South Street. Unlike Anger at Innocence except for locale, the novel has dominant Black characters as only one white plays a significant role.

South Street is the story of three adult brothers, Claude, Michael, and Philip Bowers, who have entirely different philosophies and lifestyles. Smith introduces additional characters who have merely functional roles. Vulgarity—not for the sake of shock or sensationalism—plus violence and a love story are the basic ingredients of his third novel. This work was the first in a trilogy that Smith envisioned, to be followed by "Simeon" and "The Gangsters."[47] The latter two were never published, and manuscripts indicating the plots of each were lost or misplaced.[48] As in Anger at Innocence, Smith allows coincidence in certain portions of the novel to mar the story. South Street is, however, a story that moves swiftly, as Smith's craftsmanship overcomes even those deficits.

The novel begins on a hot Saturday in July on South Street, where many people move slowly in the unbearable steaming weather. Slim, a numbers runner, enters a bar for a drink; later he goes to a nightclub looking for Lil, his girlfriend, who works there as a waitress. The club has an oval bar with enough room in the center to permit a "four-piece band and the Blues Singer" to perform. He notices the Old Man sitting at a table with Margaret and the three Bowers brothers. Slim asks if anyone has seen Lil; the Old Man tells him she just went out. Philip and Michael are seen often by Slim, but Claude has not been around for years. Claude and Slim talk; Claude tells him he has been back for a week after being in Africa for two years, "fighting . . . for Africa's freedom!"

The happy group is very playful. At intermission the Blues Singer greets Claude with a kiss. Lil walks in with a man "close behind her" and goes to the bar. Minutes later she walks over to the group seated at a table. She greets Slim "with a sugared, slightly drawled voice" and sits next to Claude, asking, "And who is this lovely man?" Michael introduces her to Claude, who is a bit embarrassed at her overly sensous approach.

On Sunday morning Michael accompanies an old widow to church; he later visits the Old Man at his home. He questions the politically connected Old Man, who says he is satisfied with his job as a committeeman and the "pleasant company of young ladies." Michael is not impressed and asks if he has a "purpose." The Old Man advises him to "analyze the world, then find out how you can make your way inside of it." Michael wonders aloud how the Old Man can "be happy while Negroes are so unhappy." The Old Man responds: "Negroes are not unhappy, son. That's a myth created by Richard Wright."[49] Michael snaps: "We don't want revenge. We want to fight for what's right!" pausing to realize that the Old Man "had achieved what he thought was success." He leaves to meet Claude.

Philip's Sunday is spent with Margaret; they have dinner and later go to the movies. Taking her home later, he proposes they get engaged. She says she cannot accept his offer because she loves Claude, confirming Philip's suspicions.

Michael and Claude, meanwhile, pass a church from which the sound of a violin is emanating. Claude listens, then walks to the church wall to read: "Kristin Kennedy, Young Violinist in Recital, Wednesday, July 20." Claude returns to the church for the recital. He enjoys the music of the young artist and later goes backstage to congratulate her on the performance. Afterwards, at a nearby store, he stops for coffee only to meet her again when she enters minutes later. They sit discussing music several minutes as several white boys stare in surprise and astonishment at the interracial couple. After finishing coffee, she drives him home and gives him her address, asking that he visit her on Friday. He agrees, but fails to meet her. The following day Kristin goes to Claude's home and is met by Philip. Claude appears and apologizes for missing the visit. Playfully, she demands that he visit the studio, "Now! This minute!" Once there they listen to music and talk about their backgrounds: Kristin has studied music for years; Claude mentions his father's death and that he presently writes a weekly article for a Black newspaper.

Slim's job as a numbers runner is controlled by a Mafia type named Pete. He tells Pete that the runners in his district want a raise so that their pay equals what he is paying the white runners. Pete says that no one gets more than the others; Slim tells him the Black runners will go on strike. Pete reminds him if they strike there "might be bodies floatin' down the river." Slim leaves without further comment and returns to his apartment, where Lil waits. He tells her how he made out with Pete. Later they make love.

Claude increases his visits to Kristin. One day Gordon, her white accompianist, arrives while Claude is at the studio and, after his initial shock, warms up and joins their conversation; it occurs to Claude later that Gordon is in love with her.

In late August, as Michael and Philip leave a movie theater, they encounter a white crowd surrounding a Black man who is quarreling with a white man; the men are close to fighting. Michael watches the events as Philip worries about what might happen if the fight explodes in to a free-for-all. They watch and listen to the would-be combatants. Michael hears the white man use "foul profanity." He "stepped through the crowd . . .

[and] stood in front of the startled, drawn-white face and struck with all his force. The man, shocked, fell to the ground. Blood flowed from the mouth and the nose of the man; he stared up, shocked, unmoving at Michael" (p. 56). He leaves the scene with Philip beside him. At home Philip ponders a personal question: "Am I a coward?" He is the most sensitive of the brothers and the weakest. "In the face of violence . . . fear . . . always" is his constant companion. His question is answered in this realization.

Michael's reaction to striking the white man is the complete opposite; his only thought: "At the first hint of violence, at the first show of hate, strike a blow! Afterwards, die. Do not wait. Do not think. Trust the impulse. Strike the blow! He had struck the blow" (p. 58). But Michael is not without fear; only Claude is totally without fear, he feels. America is a land of many faces; it is the "Land of Klansman . . . Land of the Hypocrite. . . . his own father, who had been a Man; whipped; his entrails cut out; then shot because, in a Southern town, he had been the first who had dared to vote" (p. 59).

Claude, meanwhile, is often with Kristin. She asks him what he does in his spare time; he tells her about the nightclub. She becomes excited and wants to go there. Claude agrees to take her there. At the nightclub she stands out because of her white skin; moreover, she is with Claude. Michael is visibly agitated by their arrival; he believes she is a psuedoliberal and verbally attacks her. Claude stops him in a sharp voice. Kristin is bewildered as Claude takes her home. Several hours later he returns to the nightclub and announces that he and Kristin will be married the following week. Directing his words to Michael, he adds: "You're invited . . . if you'd like to come." Michael stares at Claude and says nothing, but in his eyes burns something close to hate.

Smith ends the first section of the book with the major characters introduced. His characterization of Michael—as an earlier version of the late Malcolm X—is extremely interesting, and it should be noted that Smith developed the character of Michael years before the appearance of Malcolm X on the national and international scene. South Street was the first novel that can clearly be called the "militant protest novel."[50]

In Book Two, "Neighbors," Claude marries Kristin and travels to Montreal on their honeymoon. Returning to their hometown, they move into her studio. Development of other characters in the novel are of more than passing interest: The Blues Singer, shy about her nudity, wants to find a woman to love and later meets a young lesbian; the Old Man continues his pursuit of young ladies although, in one situation, his scheme backfires; Lil finds a room away from her family; while Claude and Kristin meet another interracial couple, Dan and Suzette Johnson. At a restaurant they are insulted by a group of white men. One of them says: "Well, will you look at these goddamn niggers!" Claude walks over to the man and asks him to repeat what he just said, and as the man begins, "Claude had never struck a man so hard. All the strength of his body and all of his anger were thrown against the man's face. The man fell to the floor, instantly unconscious" (p. 129). A larger fight is averted; they complete dinner and leave.

Smith's characters continue to resort to violence. He combines themes of love, hate, race, violence, Black, white, "coward-type" men, brazen women, artists, writers, young, and old as material to explore. Some of his personal traits appear in several characters, although it is hard to identify a composite of him in any particular character. His ability to incorporate bits and pieces of his personal philosophy into his fictional characters is very interesting. In the semiautobiographical Last of the Conquerors, parts of Smith are detectable in Hayes Dawkins; Theodore Hall of Anger at Innocence, who aspires to be a writer and also disliked his father shows a more striking similarity to Smith's own life. Moreover, the character of Juarez, a Third World intellectual, is similar to Smith. Dawkins's employment in a "photo store" and Theodore Hall's working in a "photographic supplies store" as a salesman seem to refer to Smith's early employment.

"Festival," the third part of the novel, explores three days of the event as a backdrop for the characters' activities. The best and worst in their personalities appear: Kristin gets caught up in the merriment; Philip, since joining Michael's Negro Action Society, has become completely open and receptive to the group's endeavors. Lil attends the affair; Michael appears at the celebration with Margaret; and Claude is questioned about his marriage by some old friends as the first night's activities end.

On the second day the Old Man is "in his glory" surrounded "by a bevy of beautiful girls." Lil is in a bar on South Street; she later does an impromptu dance, exciting the spectators. Margaret accidentally meets Claude away from the crowd and almost allows her emotions to betray her, but Michael appears. That night, Dan and his wife are walking aimlessly when they are assaulted by a group of "white youths, six or seven of them." Dan is knocked unconscious as Suzette runs back to South Street to give the alarm. Meanwhile, Lil is entertaining the crowd, dancing in a suggestive manner. Slim notices her inebriated state and, hurt by her cheap conduct, picks up a prostitute and pays for her services in a nearby squalid room. Returning to the street, he is shocked when Lil holds her "skirt above her knees," still dancing on the platform. He seizes her and carries her to street level, where he is halted by Pete. He puts her down and argues with him. Suzette appears and screams to the crowd what has happened to Dan. Claude and a large group of revelers return to where Dan is, "bruised and bloody." A gang of Black youths and Michael want to "visit" the area where the white youths live. Claude tries to restrain them; Michael tells him he is a "coward." Michael and the youths leave to revenge the assault.

Smith keeps the pace of South Street moving swiftly with jealous lovers, mayhem, drugs, and music in an almost maddening succession. He employs flashback techniques for several characters, yet weaves it into the fabric of the overall plot in a convincing and inconspicuous fashion.

Lil, rescued from Slim by Pete, winds up going to his apartment. Claude sits in a bar talking to the Blues Singer about the events of the assault on Dan. Margaret waits for Michael at another bar; he later shows up with a "slight bruise under one eye." He tells her they "got a lot of them." Slim questions himself about Lil's conduct and wonders: "Why?"

The following day the tone of the festival has changed. A different kind of crowd, smaller than the previous two days' outpouring, appears on South Street. The Old Man is there to judge the choir contest; the Blues Singer gets up and surprises the audience by singing a hymn. Nearby the Negro Action Society holds a gathering with Michael, the founder and featured speaker. He delivers a stunning address on "The Negro—Past and Present." (The speech is reminiscent of Malcolm X's lectures during the early 1960's.) As the audience is leaving, Slim's nephew, bleeding, is half-carried into the hall; the white boys have avenged the retaliatory assault by Michael and the youths of South Street.

In Book Four, "Rain," the marriage of Claude and Kristin suffers because of the fast-moving racial events at the festival. Tension and fighting between Blacks and whites escalate as the Negro Action Society becomes inactive due to the organization's "lack of faith" in Michael's leadership. Meanwhile, Lil is enjoying herself in the company of different men since her romance with Slim has ended. Her affair with Pete grows. He secures a new apartment for her and makes demands on her that she does not agree with. He tells her she belongs to him. She smiles and tells him, "Cars and apartments don't buy me, my sweet. Lil belongs . . . to Lil! To nobody else!" (p. 212).

Smith continues building tensions as Philip, awed by the display of the Action Society and his own cowardice, leaves the group and returns to his former nonviolent nature. Claude and Michael meet one night, and Michael urges him to lead the Society. Claude has another problem: His marriage is beginning to erode.

Book Five, "Cymbals," is the concluding section. It begins with the Old Man in a panic about his political future. His dilemma is that the man his party supports will lose, so he decides to switch sides on order to become a magistrate, the promised political reward for his delivery of votes. Lil, meantime, continues enjoying herself, much to Pete's dismay. He warns her about flirting. Kristin and Claude, to avoid racial incidents, stay at home, becoming tense and nervous. Philip, meanwhile, is working in a lending library, where he meets Raye. A very attractive woman, she pursues a graduate degree at night and wants to be a writer; after a whirlwind courtship, they become engaged.

Slim is now a bartender, having quit the numbers job. He has a new girlfriend, as Lil continues entertaining Pete. Claude and Kristin still suffer with bouts of "moodiness"; but when Claude, seeking a solution to ongoing problems, mentions divorce to her, she is shocked. Several nights later he asks her, "Why couldn't we live in Montreal?"

The Blues Singer becomes a drug addict after trying heroin. She reflects on her life and realizes it is empty: "That was the Blues (p. 288). Margaret, meanwhile, is becoming disillusioned with Michael and the Action Society; he realizes that he is too serious about his commitments and remains quiet, as he agrees with her negative assessment of him. Philip, on the other hand, is at Raye's apartment. They are discussing their plans for marriage. Raye used to think that she would "never love anybody." But she loves him and when he "kissed her . . . both of them trembled. He had never been with a woman before. Nor had she been with a man. They went cleanly to each other. They were gentle; they were tender; they were romantically in love" (p. 296).

A drunken Pete arrives at Lil's apartment talking about "those goddam niggers!" out on strike. He apologizes to Lil for the derogatory remark and tells her he's had Slim "fixed" via a beating. Lil stares at him, then attemps to leave. Pete slaps her hard, and she falls to the floor; her eyes blaze and she gets up, saying nothing. Pete later kisses her and invites her to bed.

> The blaze had gone from her eyes now; they were soft and surrendering. She put her arms around his neck, locked the arms behind his head.
>
> He lowered his lips to hers. Her lips parted. There was a razor between her teeth.
>
> Pete screamed. Lil's arms were locked behind his head. She held him tight. Her eyes shone hatred. Holding him tight, she moved her head from side to side (p. 299).

Lil's revenge for the assault Pete ordered on Slim is complete; she has never stopped loving Slim. She leaves Philadelphia by train for California, but meets a businessman en route and decides to go to Chicago with him.

For several weeks Claude and Kristin pack, store, and arrange to sell the studio, anticipating the trip to Canada. While their plans move forward, a happy Philip walks down a street near the Black-white border of Grays Ferry; he would never know "the stone was in the air," thrown by a disgruntled white youth, "beaten savagely" months earlier by rampaging Black youngsters. "The stone struck Philip at the temple. A jagged edge cut through into the vein. Philip fell. Blood poured from the vein. . . . Philip lay on the pavement, his face in the pool made by his own blood" (pp. 303-4).

Meanwhile, a happy Claude and excited Kristin looked at the almost empty studio. Abruptly, "there was a knock on the door; . . . Kristin opened the door" to see a "panting dark youth" who said he wanted to talk to Claude. He tells Claude, "I was sent here by your brother Michael, Claude. I got a message. It ain't a pretty message. I was sent to tell you that your brother Philip is dead" (p. 304). The boy explains the circumstances of Philip's death to a shocked Claude and Kristin. Claude goes to the morgue with Michael to identify the body, and then both return to the studio. Kristin is told that a possible riot stemming from Philip's death has been averted by Claude's addressing the would-be rioters. Michael apologizes to Kristin for his past conduct and treatment; Claude later takes Kristin to the hotel where they were to spend the night before leaving for Canada. He leaves her there and returns to South Street, thinking about Philip. His intellect helps him understand the ironies and ways of the world as his marriage is finished; racism has claimed new victims.

The novel ends where it began, at the nightclub. The Old Man is at his favorite table savoring the congratulations from many for being a winner in the election. The Old Man would be a magistrate! In the midst of his happiness

> The lights dimmed. . . . The people became quiet. The Blues Singer mounted the platform, under the spotlight. The light flickered from her sequins.
>
> The Blues Singer threw back her head and opened her mouth and began to sing (p. 312).

And South Street ends with that scene.

The novel demonstrates the growing maturity of Smith as a writer. The complexities of writing a plot with as many characters and maintaining the action and interplay between them are extremely engaging. Certain characters, possibly the Old Man, Michael, Claude, or the Blues Singer could have been explored further; this is what Smith apparently wanted to do with the Old Man. In the nonpublished "Simeon" manuscript the old, corrupt politician character may have been a further extension of the Old Man.[51] Moreover, Michael might have resorted to criminal activities as a character in another nonpublished manuscript, "The Gangsters."

South Street is a very interesting and moving novel, giving insight into the lifestyle of certain Afro-Americans during the late 1940s or 1950s. The novel, however, was greeted with mixed criticism. Henry F. Winslow, commenting in Crisis, wrote, "In South Street Mr. Smith's choice of a wide variety of characters . . . is made at the sacrifice of depth in any one. Nevertheless, the author's touch, though not firm, is sure; for here is a high fidelity recording of sights and sounds in Philadelphia and similar communities."[52] Writing in the New York Times Book Review, Gilbert Millstein wrote, "There are the usual and justifiable detailings of the white man's brutality, both physical and spiritual, toward the black man; the customary reminders that Negroes suffer not simply because they are Negroes but because they are human as well. The whole thing is earnest, accurate and wooden."[53] Doris Dungill Holmes, writing in Pylon said, "South Street . . . is stimulating. Although its concentration is not fresh, its treatment is impressive; and you will not relax while reading it—nor does this reviewer think that William Gardner Smith wants you to do so."[54]

Maturing in Europe 4

The year 1954 thrust Smith into the third year of his absence from the United States. Several things made the year memorable, chief among them his employment with Agence France-Presse (AFP), the news service branch of the French government. Smith explained in a letter to his mother, "I am a desk editor. . . . and my job is to translate and rewrite in English the stories which originally come in in French. I work six hours per day, six days per week, for a salary of slightly more than $200 per month."[1] While the position at AFP would sustain him, together with the limited monies received from the publication of South Street, he summed up his stay in Paris since 1951 in a interview:

> When my money ran out . . . I heard about a job at a French news service for an American. I applied for it by phone and I said to myself, "When they see me, that's the end." Back in the States I took civil service typing tests. I was fast and I was accurate, but I was never called.
>
> I went down to the office and took a test. They gave me a story in French and asked me to make an American story out of it in English. I finished it and the Frenchman said, "There's nothing right now, but come in on Friday." I didn't. On Saturday the man called me and wanted to know what happened. He had a job. I started on Monday.[2]

In speaking of his writing during the first years in Paris he added, "I was still emotionally in the States and I was writing along a line started a long time ago. But while I was writing about the past, I was undergoing what you call 'an agonizing reappraisal' of myself and what I wanted to write. That's one of the reasons I took the job with the news service. I had come to a dead end. I felt I couldn't go down the old road any longer. I mean the road of protest."[3]

Meanwhile, Smith's social life would keep its exciting pace.

He continued living at the Hôtel Tournon. He met a woman several years older than himself, Musy Hafner, who had a young son. They were to live at the hotel for quite some time although the room they shared was almost crumbling; at one point the ceiling threatened to fall upon them. The owner merely propped up supports to keep the ceiling from falling.[4] Smith would remain in the downstairs cafe until the wee hours of the morning, at times with Joshua Leslie, a black Jamaican-American, discussing politics. Leslie, who was attending the Sorbonne and doing graduate work to complete his doctorate, was later to become a brilliant mathematician.[5]

During another period, "at the Café Le Tournon . . . a highly-animated group of Black Americans sat drinking coffee, beer or cognac." Smith describes the scene:

> It was a raw winter in 1954, and the garish green, red, and white cafe, with its hideous paintings of Luxembourg Gardens on the walls, was warm and cozy. . . . The blacks gathered there included writers Richard Wright, Chester Himes, and James Baldwin, artists Ollie Harrington and Larry Potter, actor Gordon Heath, jazz musician Art Simmons, and orchestra conductor Dean Dixon.[6]

Among the group of expatriates was Smith, who had published his third novel earlier in the year.

The work at Agence France-Presse was interesting; Smith's command of the French language was improving manyfold, after an abortive start at the Alliance Francaise, the French language school, where he decided the pace of learning the language was too slow.[7] His hours at AFP were from 6 p.m. until midnight, and he was consistently nocturnal.[8] He met all sorts of people in his nightly prowls: the bright, witty, political, beautiful, and ugly. The Algerian War was in its early stages; somewhere in his later travels around Paris he became involved in the Algerian goal of "Algeria-for-Algerians.[9]

"For a long while I have not written anything, because the publisher's turned down my last book, and I wanted to rest awhile and think. I just [do] my job at the office. . . . Now, I want to start a new book."[10] So wrote Smith to his mother in mid-June 1955, although he had published South Street the previous year. The book he referred to as being turned down was a novel titled "Simeon," probably written during 1953.[11] Although a copy of the manuscript is not available—it was lost—the following is known about the novel:

> "Simeon" is the story of a young man who meets an older man—a businessman or lawyer—who wants to show Simeon the tricks of the trade of politics. The older man's motto is based on " you have to be corrupt enough to produce." Simeon is very talented and very pure and is torn between being pure and not compromising his

principles and succeeding in life rather by scrupulous means. Interwoven in the story is another person, because "Simeon" is also a love story.[12]

Moreover, "the late J. Austin Norris, machiavellian Republican politician, powerbroker, attorney. . . as well as Bill's nemesis, is undoubtedly 'the Old Man' of the lost, unpublished 'Simeon.'"[13] Additionally, Smith had "already been making notes for the third [and concluding book] of the 'South Street' series."[14] In writing to his publisher and sometimes editor, John Farrar, Smith wanted to know if a decision on publication of "Simeon" had been reached because he wanted "to receive $500 which is due on delivery of the manuscript."[15] But one early reaction to the manuscript had already been received by the publishers. It said, "SIMEON has flavor, but I think it fails as a story, and never produces a sympathetic affinity between the reader and the characters. Perhaps editing and cutting would benefit the manuscript, but I don't want to make a commitment on the basis of the present draft.[16] Finally, after receiving similar responses from other readers, John Farrar concluded that "it is a perfectly good story although . . . it needs a tremendous amount of work."[17] Farrar went on to say, "I am afraid Bill has lost the magic again. Particularly after working on SOUTH STREET, that book's quality just doesn't seem to be in SIMEON."[18] Smith, meantime, "had been trying hard to polish the first section of a new novel, THE GANGSTERS, in order to send it in and get a new contract."[19] The manuscript of "The Gangsters," like "Simeon," suffered the same fate; it was lost and, unlike "Simeon," the story, characters, and details are unknown.[20]

In a letter addressed to his mother, Smith spoke of several aspects of his living in Paris:

> I don't know what you must have thought of me all these months—whether I was ill, unhappy, or worse. I was here all the time, and in good health. Sometimes I was extremely broke, but nothing ever became more serious than that.
>
> I am the only Negro at the agency [AFP], and the people there are wonderful. I have a month vacation each year (I've only been there a year, and this will be my first vacation).
>
> You asked when I was coming home. I don't know. First of all, I would need money for a two-way trip—which is very expensive. . . . I may be home for a visit next year, when I have my vacation—provided I have the money. But I shall not stay in the States.
>
> When I think of the States, it seems to me that I'm thinking of a foreign country. Paris is more familiar to me, it seems. When I feel at all even like visiting the States, it is only because of you and the family. I love all of you and would like to see you again, and talk to you, and see how everybody has changed. But there is nothing else that I want there.

> This opinion becomes reenforced everytime a friend of mine goes back to the States and writes to me to give his impressions. Everyone is sad to go back, everyone would like to stay over here. I was lucky to find a job, for the French don't want to give their jobs to foreigners—they don't have enough for the French.
>
> The people are poor, and nearly all of us (foreigners) live in rooms we would never live in in the States. But life takes on a different meaning here, and things like that don't count very much.
>
> Remember Richard Gibson? He used to come around and see me sometime, before I got married. (He still went to see me afterward. . . .). Well, he is here, and he says that he has nightmares whenever he thinks that he might have to go back to the States to stay. I am trying to get a job for him at that agency, but they don't need anyone right now and I don't know if I'll finally succeed.[21]

Gibson had arrived in Europe during the summer of 1951; he was there to study at the University of Rome. In 1952 he visited Paris to be with Mary and Smith, but Mary had already departed for the States. Returning to Italy, Gibson was drafted into the US Army in Trieste in December 1952. He managed to get himself stationed in West Germany and secured three-day-pass trips to Paris after first completing basic training at Fort Dix, New Jersey. Discharged from the army in late 1954, Gibson headed straight for Paris, where he studied at the Sorbonne on GI educational benefits.[22] Reflecting on this period, Gibson says,

> In the summer of 1955, Bill. . . . introduced me to Jacques Lapine, one of the directors of the English service [at AFP], and Lapine eventually offered me a job there. . . . It was exacting if eventually dull work, but I was glad to have it. If it had not been for Bill, I doubt if I would have got the job. We were the only blacks on the staff, but I never saw any instance of racism from anyone there at any time during the three years I worked at AFP. . . . They all liked Bill very much and his job at AFP was a secure one.[23]

By now, Smith was "living with a . . . woman. . . . She was an actress and had been married to an East German Communist leader. She had a son by her German husband . . . and had hoped to marry [Smith]."[24] On March 24, 1956, Gibson married his English girlfriend, Joy Marguerite Kaye (familiarly known as Sarah), with Smith as best man.[25]

Meanwhile, in the world at large, life moved on at its normal pace of threats of aggression, births, murders, changes of weather, movement of individual life, and so on. More important, "the beginnings of the Algerian War in 1954 and 55 hardly were noticed by foreigners in Paris."[26] "We at AFP," Gibson remembers, "read the dispatches from Algiers about 'bandits' and 'outlaws,' but it was hard to realize that this was a major anti-imperialist revolution."[27] And by now the Paris office of the US Department of State had failed to renew Smith's passport. But he remained in Paris, officially a "stateless" person.[28] Exactly why and when Smith's passport was taken or invalidated is not known. What is known is that he had his passport during 1954 and that when he traveled to East Germany with Musy Hafner and her son in 1955, his passport was in his possession.[29]

The new year, 1957, began with Smith and Musy's still living together, while back in Philadelphia—after exchanging several letters requesting Smith sign the necessary papers for a "desertion and mutual consent" divorce decree—Mary finally received his signature of agreement. The divorce became final during January.[30] On February 6 Smith was thirty years old.

The Algerian War had escalated by this time, with the French doing their best to quell the disturbance in their North African colony. Ugly scenes were taking place daily in the French capital with some of the foreigners or the expatriates—especially those with political leanings—either taking a position with the host country, France, or, affiliating themselves with the Algerians. Smith had chosen to side with the Algerians. This choice was in direct conflict with his expatriate status as a "guest"; as such, he was not supposed to involve himself with the politics of France. For whatever reasons Smith chose as he did, this was his position in 1957, probably earlier. Before the year was over Smith, Richard Gibson, Ollie Harrington, and Richard Wright found themselves the leading participants in a situation that would eventually be called "the Gibson Affair."[31]

Earlier in the year Smith had applied for a passport at the American Embassy in Paris. Before issuance or approval of the passport he had to complete a sworn statement that included the questions "Are you now a member of the Communist Party?" and "Have you ever been a member of the Communist Party?" Smith responded in the negative to both questions.[32] And on the same day he filed a sworn deposition stating,

> Under protest, I today signed an affidavit at the American Embassy at Paris, France to the effect that I am not now or ever have been a member of the Communist Party.
>
> I am a professional writer, journalist and a member of the Executive Committee of a Negro organization [The Philadelphia Branch of] the National Association for the Advancement of Colored People. In these capacities I came into contact and know Communists, Trotsky-ites, Democrats, Republicans, etc. In my capacity as writer I was associated with the Philadelphia Council of the Arts, Sciences and Professions. In my capacity as a newspaper reporter and a member of a Negro organization I was frequently associated with the Civil Rights Congress and I had contact with the Socialist Workers Party and even once wrote an article published in one of their newspapers.

> I am today applying for a new passport to enable me to travel in connection with my writing. At the present time I am planning to travel to Italy, Spain and Ghana.[33]

After a "please give anything since 1951" request to the FBI from the embassy, the response from the Washington, D.C., office of the State Department "concluded that his case does not come within the provisions of Section 51.135 of the Passport Regulations at the present time," and Smith was issued a new passport on August 7, 1957.[34]

The Gibson Affair had its origins during the summer of 1956 when Gibson "had rented [Ollie Harrington's] Paris studio" when Harrington left Paris.[35] It is said that "Harringtion was disagreeably surprised on his return to find that Gibson not only refused to vacate the apartment, but claimed to own the furniture, paintings and personal belongings that [Harrington] had left behind."[36] Gibson counters that statement by saying that Harrington "was broke and urgently needed money. He owed hundreds of thousands of (old) francs in back (unpaid) rent to Raymond Duncan, the landlord. He did not own any of the furniture and there were no paintings in the one-room flat. [Harrington] had no legal title and Duncan refused to have him back unless he paid what he owed. . . . The French police and courts would have found that Harrington had no case and he know it."[37] This heated argument would remain the center of each man's immense dislike of the other for quite some time.

Harrington found living quarters in another part of Paris "rather than call in the police, fearing that the American Embassy might intervene on account of his status as an expatriate with Communist sympathies."[38] While this might have been Harrington's cover story to his cronies, the plausibility of that statement does not ring true. Why would Harrington so easily allow his apartment and its contents—allegedly his own—to be taken?

In the meantime, Smith "would not disavow his friend [Gibson], with the result that the Black community had slowly taken sides in the struggle."[39] How long Smith maintained his alleged position is a matter of speculation in that within a year a person who met Smith at Café Le Tournon stated: "When I met Bill [in 1957], his best friend was . . . Harrington. . . . He was a father to Bill. . . .Bill [and Gibson] were not on speaking terms. [Gibson] had had a quarrel with Ollie. Bill was on Ollie's side."[40] Harrington found immediate support for his position with Richard Wright, "who had been his good friend since his arrival in [1952?]."[41] But events were building—situations that would see personalities scarred, strengths and weaknesses of the individuals concerned become apparent, and friendships permanently ended.

During the period Smith found enough time to write two magazine articles, "Master of the Sex Story" and "Europe's Naked Nature Boy." Both articles were published by an American girlie magazine, with French author Guy de Maupassant the subject of

"Master of the Sex Story,"[42] and Manneken-Pis, the famous bronze statue in Brussels, the topic of "Europe's Naked Nature Boy."[43]

The Gibson Affair—Smith is credited with giving the situation its name—continued to grow in intensity, each side claiming its own righteousness.[44] Almost abruptly, the matter was brought to a head. In Life magazine, the issue of September 30, 1957, on the editorial page, there appeared an article entitled "Hopeful Plan for Algeria."[45] Three issues later, Life published the following in its letters to the editor section:

> Life maintains that there will be political and economic chaos in Algeria when France is finally forced to give up her colonial holdings ("Hopeful Plan for Algeria," Life, Sept. 30). The chaos, Life forgot to mention, is right here in France. Any American who thinks that France of her own will, will grant Algeria, if not independence, at least some liberal status where seven million Algerians will not be crushed politically by a million Europeans is mad. Ollie Harrington, Paris, France.[46]

Additionally, "similar letters were also sent to The Observer in London . . . that appeared on January 20 and January 30, 1958. Harrington, however, had not written the letters."[47] Upset by this turn of events and knowing that "the French policy was to deport any foreigner who got involved with French deomestic politics . . . [Harrington] initiated an investigation with the support of the well-known criminal lawyer Jacques Mercier" to resolve the legal entanglements.[48]

Gibson came under immediate suspicion because of the studio apartment incident and his subsequent alienation from the expatriates; moreover, who else would want Harrington deported? Gibson explains:

> Bill agreed in principle, but worried about possible arrest and expulsion from France. Nevertheless, he agreed that something should be done to help the Algerians and we hatched a very hairbrained [sic] scheme to send letters to U.S. and British publications, denouncing French colonialism and supporting the Algerians. Bill was to get the approval of other blacks in Paris—Richard Wright, Chester Himes, Ollie Harrington, the cartoonist. . . . The idea was to write letters, signing the names of others and each in turn would deny, if asked by French authorities, that the letter was by him. The denials would probably not be printed, we thought, in any case and the Algerian cause would be served.
>
> Bill suggested that I write in the name of Ollie Harrington. This surprised me because Harrington and I had had a bitter (and physical) fight over an apartment on the Rue de Seine. Nevertheless I went ahead, wrote

> the letter and told Bill. . . . Anyway, in no time at all, I was arrested by French police on a complaint by Harrington who rightly protested that I had forged his name. The police astounded me by informing me that Bill Smith had provided them with proof that I was the forger. When I was immediately released by the police, Bill was in consternation. He protested to the management of AFP about my presence on the staff and I was fired.[49]

And "the French and American Police [had] found conclusive evidence that Gibson had written the letters."[50] Gibson states that "as far as I know, no 'American police' were involved in the case of the letters, but I was picked up by the DST [French counterpart of America's FBI or CIA], who had a full file on me and my contacts and samples of my writing, etc., which they said all had come from Bill Smith."[51] Gibson continues, "They showed me a signed statement from Bill. Although I had been working side by side with him through all that period, he had never said one word or warned me, which seems the least anyone would do."[52]

Shortly after the forgery situation was exposed, several things happened that caused Gibson to sign a confession. He says: "I was told that it was better to sign a confession, leaving out all mention of politics—this from the DST—and to write a letter of apology to Harrington, which was dictated by his lawyer."[53] "In return," Gibson continues, "I was to be allowed to stay in France."[54] But, before the confession, "a memorable fight ensued in the Café de Tournon, where Harrington thrashed [Gibson] so thoroughly that [he] had to be taken to the hospital."[55]

Richard Wright, however, took it upon himself to examine the Gibson Affair in detail, since, he thought, some of his own problems may have been tied up in the situation. Accordingly, he drew up a list of thirty-one questions with Smith's name appearing in twenty-three. The questions were "designed to reveal Gibson's real notives and William Gardner Smith's true position."[56] Wright "got in touch with Gibson . . . who wrote back denouncing Smith as a 'false brother' . . . but Wright thought that Smith, who was ostensibly acting as a friend, was actually attacking him, and while it was also rumored that Wright was an FBI agent, he was convinced that the CIA itself was the source of all these machinations."[57]

Of the thirty-one questions Wright directed to Gibson, the following are the reactions of Gibson that Wright noted: "Gibson first tried what he thought would excite my emotions: a racial approach"; "Gibson attempts an unsuccessful effort at talking and acting like an executive white man, yet his high-pitched tone and head ducking never allow him to measure up to his imagined standard and he is half-conscious of it"; "Gibson repeatedly said: I'm not government. But he did not say that he was not an agent and repeatedly he talked of the CIA!!!! And had a most detailed knowledge of it in Germany"; "Whatever I pushed Gibson hard about something he always found a 'personal' rather than a political reason for the action. Hence he says Bill fought him [figuratively] because he slept once with Bill's wife."[58]

The Gibson Affair, as Wright implied in one of his thirty-one questions, should have generated some attention, and it did, insofar as Frank Van Brakle, a freelance journalist, was concerned. Wright went a question further: "Why has JET or the Negro Press never carried any news of this fight?" A letter was, in fact, sent to Jet magazine; it stated:

> The story stretches all the way from a charming apartment on the romantic left-bank of Paris to the austere hall of the French Ministry of Interior. . . . The case involves forged notes to many world known publications such as Life magazine, the London Sunday Observer and the London Sunday Times attempting to involve Negro personalities living in Paris with the Algerian Rebel Organization, just two weeks "coincidentally" before this explosive issue was to be debated in the halls of the United Nations.
>
> The personalities involved in this real life cloak and dagger drama are three well known Negro authors, the outstanding Negro cartoonist in America, . . . a brilliant young Negro mathematician and his southern born wife, an outstanding physicist in her own right, both completing their PHD's at the Sorbonne, and a distinguished cancer authority, a Negro, who is a professor at an Ivy League University. The Sureté Nationale, the French equivalent of the FBI, in brilliantly unmasking the case, rank it as infamous as L'Affaire Dreyfus; it is, as a matter of fact, called L'Affaire Gibson. This story has been hushed up for many reasons as you can well imagine, not the least being the present crisis in French political life. However, also as you can imagine, a story of this magnitude will not stay buried for long.[59]

If the letter was answered or not is unknown; the story, however, was never printed in Jet or any other Black or White newspaper or periodical.

It should be noted that whereas Gibson states "and we hatched a very hairbrained [sic] scheme to send letters to U.S. and British publications," describing Smith's and his role in the forged letters fiasco, he goes on to say, "Chester Himes assured me, as did Richard Wright, that Bill had never approached him with any scheme to help Algeria. . . . If [Smith] had disagreed with what I wanted to do or had done, he should have said so."[60] Clearly, the language is of extreme importance when considering how Gibson himself assessed the situation almost twenty years later. Whereas it may be considered a slip of the tongue, one can possibly see a misintended confessional statement.[61]

The fears of all the participants in the affair clearly show the inner tensions each man experienced. The personality clashes, the possibility of being returned to America by either the French government or the United States, or the condition of being faced with semistatelessness without a valid passport seems to have weighed heavily on each one. Moreover, Wright's fears of "both Smith and Gibson in the service of the FBI" point up the psychological dilemma of possible dreadful aspects in the frightful drama.[62] Still, one wonders if the whole affair had been invoked and conducted by American intelligence sources. The alleged solidarity of Afro-Americans residing in Paris was completely broken and the grotesque pieces left were absurdly incongruous.

L'Affaire Gibson did serve a purpose of sorts. The romanticized period of Black expatriates had ended and confrontations had been made, closing the period with a newfound maturity for all concerned. The low-keyed politics that the expatriates had enjoyed at the Café Le Tournon and Café Monaco surfaced with unexpected results, and the Gibson Affair can almost be seen as the departure and starting point for several of the participants in their past and future lives. Smith's role in the situation seems one of protecting his own interests, as each participant undoubtedly did.

William Gardner Smith, in the meantime, remained at AFP, continued visiting the Café Le Tournon, and wrote. His last published article, "The World's Most Famous Nude," had appeard in the April 1957 issue of another girlie magazine.[63] In July 1957 an excerpt from Last of the Conquerors was printed in another American magazine under the title of "The Fraulein and the Private."[64] Possibly due to a now routine life with Musy Hafner, Smith was beginning to put on some weight. In 1958 he commented that in America, "one wastes too much time being angry. Life here is more natural, more leisurely. In discussions with French people, they never say, 'How do you, a Negro, see this?' They simply ask, 'How do you see it?' In Paris you forget the color of your skin."[65] The statement, reported in Time magazine, was one of several statements made by Black expatriates on life in France's capital city. Smith added that "the biggest problem I have is missing my roots. I've no intention of writing about France, much as I like France. It's not my homeland. But if I'm going to be writing about the States, something may be wrong, little nuances. I'm very far from my home."[66]

Richard Gibson, now back in America,[67] commented in the same article upon Black expatriation: "All these people are in Europe because of social and political causes which everyone knows. The bright young white boys, after the end of their Fulbright scholarships, are able to return with reasonably light hearts to the dens of Madison Avenue or the the provincial Ph.D. factories. It is still impossible for an American Negro to return to the land of his birth in the same spirit."[68]

Smith, seemingly always available for reporters or serious students who wanted to know something about the Black writer in Paris, "far from his roots on anger and protest," attracted journalist Joseph Barry of the New York Post in March 1959. He wanted to talk to Smith because of "friendship and certainty of frankness." He asked Smith how living in France affected his "writing and how much [did] writing mean" to him. Smith said,

> "It's the most important thing in my life . . . no matter what I do, if it is not writing, I feel as though I've done nothing. As for living in Paris and its effect on my writing, it's bad. So many friends in America tell me, and they're right, but I can't explain it. . . .
>
> "I'm coming out of the waiting period, the fallow period. I haven't lost my anger; I've lost the daily irritations. But I don't want to write out of anger. I don't want a book to be a cry of anguish. I want it to shed light."
>
> "Light without heat?" [Barry asked].
>
> "The heat will come from the friction of the characters . . . and the characters will be parts of me. Paris has opened up a whole world for me. This is a beginning. Not an ending."[69]

Meanwhile, his personal relationship with Musy Hafner, whom he had lived with since 1954, was nearing its final months. By the summer of 1959 they decided to end their affair.[70]

Solange Royez, whom Smith had met briefly in 1957, reentered his life quite accidentally:

> [In] September 1959 [Solange] had a room [at the] Hôtel du Midi, 47 rue Mouffetard in Paris. One day as [she] was getting ready to go to work, [she] bumped into [Smith] outside the door. [He] was living in the same hotel. He talked and talked (mainly about politics). He seemed pleased to hear [Solange] was a Communist and [they] shared a common desire to bring more justice into the world. [Solange] noticed [he] looked sensitive and nervous.[71]

By mid-October, without money and desperate, Smith searched his mind to come up with the name of a person he could ask for a loan. It is probable that the sum he wanted to borrow from acquaintances in Paris was beyond their means or they would not lend the requested amount. He finally focused his attention on Mary, his former wife, and wrote:

> It's been ages since I've written to you, and this is a shameful way to renew a correspondence. The only justification I can think of is impersonal: I am writing an excellent novel, and am entering on a period where I shall write much better ones.
>
> For five years—since "South Street," which, I learned from second hand, you did not like—I have not written a book. Everything went dry in me—because, I think, of the fact that I had cut off my roots, was no longer in the States, among people I had been born with, grown up with. But a slow frustration was growing—<u>because</u> I was not writing. And last May,

> suddenly, after five years of working there, I quit the Agence France-Presse to return to writing.
>
> Fortunately, at that time I received a letter from Fawcett Publications asking me to write a novel about a scandal in France, called the "Pink Ballets" scandal, of which you may have heard. I agreed, but soon found out, as I began writing, that the novel was much more complicated, and more profound, than I had thought. Fawcett offered an advance on royalties if I would send a part of the book; but I could not send a part (because of the constant growing of the book).
>
> The problem is simple. I'll finish the book in December. But I am flat broke and cannot live until December, unless I return to work at the Agence. Mary, do you have $300 you don't need until the end of December (or the beginning of January—there's always a delay in receiving payment)? I know I already owe you $250, and I won't even be able to pay you that until next year. But the 300 dollars I can pay in three months
>
> I know this is a shocking letter, and it may even make you angry. As I said, my only justification is that I am writing a very good book—an important book, as far as French history is concerned. I am fighting for time.
>
> I could write you a lot of things about my life here, about what I am doing—but, as I said, I would feel like a hypocrite if I included such things in this particular letter. When I feel like telling about those things, I'll write a letter in which I don't ask you to lend me money.
>
> Please forgive me. And please at least answer, even if you refuse.[72]

On October 29, 1959, thirty-odd months after their divorce and within two weeks of the date of his letter, Mary cabled the requested sum.[73] Meanwhile, Smith continued living with Solange at the Hôtel du Midi.[74] And the loan he said he would pay back in three months was, in fact, never paid.[75]

"The book on the Pink Ballets took longer to complete than I expected, but it is finished now, and I sent it off two weeks ago." So wrote Smith to Mary in Philadelphia. He went on to say, in a letter of early July 1960,

> My agent wrote me an enthusiastic letter about it, and I expect to hear from the publisher soon. Then I can send you a check for at least part of what I owe you (since I quit the Agence, more than a year ago now, I've gotten into considerable debt, despite the fact that I've been doing translations for the French radio and various publications here, as well as occasional articles . . .). I'm thinking of doing another book called "Return of a Conqueror"—a sort of sequel to "Last of the Conquerors." Meanwhile, at present, I'm doing a

> movie scenario for Nat King Cole, who wants to do a film about an American Negro in Paris.[76]

The letter contained information of his relationship with Solange and a request for Mary to send a copy of their divorce:

> I must touch on what is, for me, a ticklish—almost embarrassing—subject. I have a French girlfriend and we think there is a possibility she is pregnant. She does not believe in abortion and neither do I, ever since a woman here damaged herself permanently, physically, having an abortion of a child which was undoubtedly mine. If Solange—that's her name . . . is pregnant, I'll marry her. For that, I need a copy of the paper proving that we are divorced. For some reason, I had hoped I would never have to ask you for this; but I must do so now.[77]

The letter, which began on an up tempo, based on news of personal friends from Philadelphia vacationing is Europe, noted: "It was wonderful and amazing to see Joe and Kris Hunter [husband and wife] over here. . . . They were thrilled meeting Richard Wright and above all Chester Himes, both of whom I see frequently.[78] The neatly typed letter ended: "Let's make the effort and keep in touch with each other."

Five months later, abruptly and totally unexpectedly, Richard Wright died on November 28, 1960. The "dean of Negro writers abroad,"[79] residing in Paris since 1947 had, less than three weeks earlier, given a lecture at the American Church in Paris on November 8.[80] Smith attended Wright's funeral services at Cimetière du Père Lachaise with Musy Hafner, his companion of earlier years. It was a very cold early December day when Wright was cremated, so cold, in fact, that they were glad to leave the cemetery.[81]

Months later, in a published article, Smith wrote a remembrance of Richard Wright. In "The Compensation For The Wound," Smith wrote:

> Richard Wright was a wounded man, therefore a distorted man—that is, different from what he would have been without the wound. The wound was the result of his race and youthful poverty in hate-filled Mississippi; it cut deep—neither fame, nor money, nor 14 years in Paris where he was idolized, could heal it.
>
> I think that Richard Wright with a white skin would have been greatly inferior to what he was as a writer (and as a man); in fact, I think he may not have been a writer at all. He needed his painful subject. With a white skin, I think he would have been able to adapt to the United States: there was something very American about his attitudes, tastes and even his basic Puritanism. I think, having known him, that he might quite innocently have been a "conformist"—an attitude which is often disastrous for art.

> Wright's subject was pain and frustration—his own pain, fragmented, analysed, carried to its ultimate lengths and consequences, projected through scores of characters. He was a "guts" writer: he poured himself into each work. . . . I cannot imagine Wright calmly "inventing" stories. . . . He had to feel strongly first, then project and shape that feeling. Whenever he did not really "feel" . . . he failed.
>
> Wright's private life, like his work, was built around the fact of being a Negro. He made speeches on the Negro problem, which he always called "The White Problem"; he sought out and enjoyed the company of Negroes in Paris with whom he invariably discussed questions of race; he loved to tell "Negro jokes" and listen to "Negro music." The "self" I saw him present in gathering of white intellectuals in Paris was stiff, embarrassed, self-conscious, false. Despite his fame and the circles in which he sometimes moved, he never, thank God, became "sophisticated. . . ."
>
> On a different level, despite his unquestioned talent and fame, he was deeply hurt when a young Negro author whom he had helped wrote an article in an American magazine which unfavorably critized Wright's work.
>
> He was all in all a very complex man, youthful and yet old with pain, gay and sad, laughing and bitter, easy to approach and yet still a bit suspicious, shy and unsure of himself despite a pleasant awareness of his position in the world of letters.
>
> His particular wound blighted, in a way, his personal life, as it has blighted the lives of many others; but there is the compensation for the wound—his books, which will live beyond him.[82]

Although it had been accepted first by an American publisher, then by a French publisher, "Pink Ballets" or "Ballets Roses" was never published. The manuscript was returned to Smith, and there are no copies available. What is known is that Smith "was trying to write a book on the scandal called 'Ballets Roses' in which he described the pornographic habits of the French upper middle class leaders. Each chapter of this book was introduced by a piece of news drawn from current information, namely the regular bombings of Algerian villages during the Algerians Independence War."[83] Nevertheless, Smith began working on a new novel.[84]

He returned to work at Agence France-Presse in the spring of 1961 and, within a couple of months, took a vacation, going to the south of France. During July he was "trying finally to learn how to swim."[85] In the letter he sent to his mother, he went on to say, "I thought seriously, a year ago, of marrying a French girl—but I changed my mind [and] remained single. However, I am getting on in years—34 now—and maybe its time to settle down. We'll see." Before closing the letter, he repeated a position he had mentioned a number of times throughout his correspondence with his mother and others:

> I don't think I'd ever be able to live in the States again—there are too many things I can't stand—but I still plan to pay a visit to the States, whenever I can afford it, just to see you and the family. I'll live outside of the States, however. I visited Eastern Europe—the Communist part—and the officials suggested that I remain there, but I turned that down, too. I want to settle in a "growing" country, and I think finally I shall go to live in Africa. I'll make a visit, first, to see what country I like.[86]

The summer was not over when Smith proposed marriage to his now constant companion, Solange Royez. On October 31, 1961, just two weeks after his tenth year as an expatriate, he married her. The wedding was held in the 6th Arrondissement. They "invited only . . . [a] very few friends—about five."[87]

Smith's mother received the news of her oldest son's marriage a couple of months later. He described his wife as a

> French girl, [named] Solange, who is 25 years old. (She is a school teacher who teaches English, so she can write to you in the language.) It's hard to describe her, because I'm so close to her: the main thing is that she is more completely on my wavelength than anyone else I've ever met; she feels what I feel, believes what I believe, and what's more she's gentle and lovely. Her family lives in Megève, a fashionable ski resort in the French Alps.
>
> Solange's father was killed during the war. Her step-father is a former ski champion, and her mother makes very popular hats.

Smith mentioned that Solange and himself "are trying to make arrangements to go live in Africa—at least for a number of years. The big problem is whether we would be able to find work there. We've written to several embassies, and we'll see what we'll see."

Reminding his mother, gently, that his corresponding with her was at times sporadic and that, after eleven years abroad, he was the same little son of yesteryear, he wrote

> Sweetheart, don't take the fact that I don't write often as a sign of a diminishing of love. I am still the same person who played half-ball with Sonny in the backyard, who told invented fairy stories to Phyllis and Sydney while washing dishes, or who sold shopping bags to buy Christmas presents. Nothing will change me, or the way I feel. Only, there is some mysterious psychological wall I face every time it comes to writing letters; and I put them off indefinitely.[88]

In mid-July 1962, Solange wrote to her mother-in-law saying that Smith was "healthy-looking [and] considered one of the best journalists [at AFP and] works 6 hours a day, either in the afternoon or in the evening [and] has one day off in the week [and] still writes books."[89] The Mrs. William Gardner Smith of just eight months was planning to mail the letter the following day, but the mailman arrived before she departed. Among the correspondence received, Smith discovered a letter from his publisher. Anxious to let his mother know the good news from the publisher that they would accept the new novel, he quickly added a note to Solange's letter: "I feel in a very good mood this morning, because it's been such a long time since I published a book. I was beginning to wonder whether there would ever be a happy meeting between my writing and the publishers."[90]

Three months later he was still writing the new novel while still working the afternoon shift at AFP.[91] He commented that he was "working hard on my new book, and think it will be published next spring. It will certainly be good to be published again. For a long time I had the impression I was just writing for myself (to pile the manuscripts in the trunk, I mean!).[92]

Continuing to write during the "terribly cold winter," he now finished the new novel. It was springtime, and Solange was pregnant. Happily, Smith wrote his mother that she was to become a grandmother: "For me, the prospect of having a child is a new and wonderful experience." The good news continued,

> My book will be out in September, and I am now working on another one. I'm pleased about publication, even though I never feel the same excitement I did when the first book was published (Remember?). . . .
>
> On May 12, I am going to Ethiopia for 2 weeks. The Agence France-Presse is sending me, all expenses paid, to cover a conference of all African countries. It's really marvelous, although Solange is a bit sad (I can't take her with me).[93]

The new novel, The Stone Face, was published in the fall of 1963. His fourth novel, it is his last published work of fiction.[94] The book is divided into three parts that trace the development of Simeon Brown, an Afro-American who is the central character. The novel's setting is Paris, where Simeon arrives after almost committing murder in Philadelphia. Smith again employs his home town as the background of the protagonist, presenting the story in semiautobiographical form. The thrust of the plot centers on Simeon's search for a nonracist society; America's racism has forced his departure. Moreover, the search is for self-identity.

The Stone Face is also a study of expatriate Black American men in the City of Light. The characters that Smith created are actually disguised fellow expatriates, although he alters their personalities successfully enough that identifiable traits grafted onto several characters render them indistinguishable.[95] Smith incorporates a love story and violence, which he used quite successfully in his earlier novels. The Stone Face is the grotesque face of racism that

Simeon Brown has encountered since, as a youth, being assaulted by a white boy and left blind in one eye.

The novel begins with Brown's arrival in France. He is "just under thirty. . . . He had only one eye; a black patch covered the socket of the other. He was tall and slender, with nervous, sensitive hands." It is May 1960 as he arrives at Gare Saint-Lazare in Paris. The railroad station and immediate streets are crowded with people; he notices a group of men "with crinkly hair and skin which is not quite white but surely is not black."

He finds a room in a small hotel; he wants to remain a loner for a while to discover the boulevards and "twisting streets of the Latin Quarter." One day he attempts to strike up a conversation with a young French woman at a café; she refuses his offer of a friendly drink and his shyness, which he had overcome even to approach her, returns; a "conditioned reflex, racism," is his immediate thought. His humiliation is softened as "the young woman's face light[s] up as she jump[s] up" to greet "a tall African, black as anthracite" for whom she has been waiting.

Simeon, "an amateur painter . . . who paints for his own amusement," stands in his room, "his paintbrush at a portrait he knew he would never finish." The sketched picture is of an "inhuman face" detailing a clamped tight jaw: "The mouth was a compressed bitter line, the skin was deathly pale, the eyes were flat, fanatic, sadistic and cold. It was . . . the face of un-man, the face of discord, the face of destruction. . . . It was this face that invited him to murder" (p. 7). The sketched portrait is the "stone face."

He leaves his room for a walk, noting briefly newspaper headlines that shout, "MOSLEMS RIOT IN ALGIERS, FIFTY DEAD." He recalls his arrival at the railroad station and wonders when he passed a "middle-aged man with swarthy skin and long crinkly hair" if the man was an Algerian as his thoughts have subconsciously taken him to the Le Tournon Café.

He is greeted "by a black mountain of a man with a moon-shaped face." The man, Babe Carter, has been in Paris for ten years. After introducing themselves, the conversation turns to why both men are in Paris. Simeon tells him: "I left to prevent myself from killing a man." He asks Babe his reason for coming to France.

> Me? I came over to get out from under. . . . So one day I just said, 'Okay, feet, let's get movin', this ain't no place for me!' You and me, we ain't the only ones. There's a new Lost Generation over here, lots of dark cats from the States who're here in Paris . . . come over to get out from under that pressure, know what I mean? Ain't never going back, either (p. 10).

Simeon notices a young woman wearing dark glasses. Babe tells him the girl's name is Maria; he assures Simeon he will meet her and asks him what he did in the States. "I was a newspaper reporter," Simeon says, adding, "And you?" Rather than answer the question, Babe gives his current status: "I got a little shop, a little bookshop. Now, come inside. Meet some of the people in the café."

In the cafe are a number of young, white, American men and women. He meets Lou, a jazz trumpeter; Clyde, a frustrated Southerner; Jinx, Clyde's wife and a nymphomaniac; their six-year-old daughter, Jane; and Maria, who is "on a trip from Poland." When Simeon asks her why she wears dark glasses, she tells him, " I am becoming blind." She is scheduled to have an eye operation a few months hence; the doctors have warned her that maybe she will be blind in a few years. She wants to become an actress and attends drama school.

Simeon reflects on her statements and recalls silently his growing up in Philadelphia's slum section. In particular, he remembers the event that led to his blinding in one eye at the hands of "Chris, leader of the gang and toughest boy in their neighborhood." Chris calls out: "Hey nigger!" Simeon is terrified as Chris stands in front of him toying "with a jagged switchblade knife. . . . [His] glazed blue eyes" are almost hypnotic, dangerous. Chris's terrifying voice commands him to respond; Simeon "open[s] his eyes and look[s] pleadingly at the stone face." Then he

> fell into a kind of stupor. Dear God, Dear God, Dear God, he cried inside himself. But the prayer was interrupted by a shrieking flash of brilliant color, followed instantly by a blazing pain. He could not hear himself screaming. "Jesus, you blinded him!" a boy yelled. Simeon screamed at the peak of his voice, falling to the pavement, darkness closing in on him, his hands clutched to the place where he had once had an eye (pp. 28-29).

Babe Carter lives above his bookshop. Simeon goes there, where he meets five fellow Blacks: Gertie and Mathilda, jazz singers; James Benson, a "used to be novelist," as he describes himself; Harold, "one of the best classical composers around"; and "Doug, who was somewhat younger than Simeon" (p. 32). Babe teases Doug that he is a "government agent" because he works as "a minor clerk in the Embassy."

The following week Babe and Simeon take a couple of Swedish girls to a club where a fight nearly ensues after four white Americans insult them; the manager of the club orders the white Americans to leave. As they leave the club later, they witness a policeman clubbing a man, "probably an Arab."

In Simeon's second flashback of import, he is halted by two policemen for being in a white neighborhood. Insulted by the derogatory term "boy," he tells the policeman: "I been looking for your sister!" The cop slaps him; Simeon punches the cop, sending him "sprawling." Arrested for assault, he is sadistically beaten by the policemen at the police station, particularly by Mike, who "pound[s] his stomach and groin," then beats him with a rubber hose. "Seeing in a flash the hard mouth and sadistic eyes . . . Simeon thought: *It's the same face!*

The illusion lasted an instant only" (p. 42).

A large group, including Simeon and Maria, decide to spend a night in a forest south of Paris. They "roast lamb over an open fire and listen to guitars until morning." The merriment continues through the night; before dawn they return to Paris with another couple. Once there, he asks her to stay with him; she agrees.

The following night he goes to a "small dingy café" with Harold. The place is filled with Arabs and Algerians. It is a strange place for Simeon, as there are no women there. Harold explains, "The women are at home with their families in Algeria. The men come here to find work and send money home." Later, when Harold goes home, Simeon visits another bar. There he notices a Dutch girl; she smiles at him, then leaves. As he leaves the bar, he sees a couple struggling nearby; the Dutch girl is arguing with a man. She cries out for help, and Simeon tells the man to leave her alone. A verbal fight ensues until it is stopped by "police brandishing tommy guns." They are arrested, and at the police station the Algerian man explains that the girl had stolen his month's pay several nights earlier. The police sergeant decides to jail the man and release Simeon.

Months prior—in Philadelphia—Simeon had glanced at a group of sailors as he sat with Charlotte, a young white girl and fellow reporter, in an all-white bar. He is attacked by the sailors who

> rushed forward, cursing and swinging at Simeon. Rage burned with the pain in Simeon's head, and as he looked at the nearest sailor, the hallucination returned: <u>It was the stone face! It was Chris-Mike</u>. He leaped free of the sailors and drew the pistol he always carried now. He looked at them, at their suddenly frightened faces, smiled, and pulled the trigger.
>
> The gun jammed. The sailors, the barman, and all the customers stared at him in amazement. "Let's get out of here," Charlotte whispered. She ran to the door while Simeon, the gun pointed toward the sailors, backed swiftly out of the bar (p. 54).

Late one afternoon a voice shouts to Simeon, "Hey! How does it feel to be a white man?" Turning, he sees four Algerians at a nearby café. The English-speaking man repeats, "Well? How does it feel?" Simeon shrugs as the man launches into a tirade telling him that he served in the Free French Navy during the war and that he spent time in America and understood what "<u>niggers</u>" meant. Ending his profusion of words, he asks: "How does it feel to be the white man for a change?" Simeon shakes his head as the Algerian continues, "We're the niggers here! Know what the French call us—<u>bicot, melon, raton, nor'af</u>. That means <u>nigger</u> in French" (p. 57).

Part Two, "The White Man," moves swiftly as Maria awaits the eye operation. Simeon wants her to move into his studio; she is reminded of someone in her past as "she look[s] at the unfinished portrait of the monstrous white face, which Simeon had propped on the easel." She explains her background as a child prisoner with a German officer during World War II. She "was nine years old, " she says, adding, "It was not exactly that he made love to me; he had—odd tastes. I was ashamed" (p. 76).

Smith introduces Ahmed, who tells Simeon he was with the man who had called him a "white man." Ahmed is a student who says the FLN [Algerian National Liberation Front] "tells me I must get my education, they will need trained men when Algeria becomes free." The next day they meet at a bus stop and go to the northern part of the city, to an area that is populated by Algerians, Arabs, and other North Africans. Simeon's thoughts turn briefly to South Philadelphia, "feeling the old unbearable frustration and anger, the fear and defiance" of the ghetto. Smith, via Simeon, reflects on a character in South Street: "Arab music assailed them from all sides. The Blues. Where was the Blues Singer now?"[96]

Ahmed explains that his family members are "traders," and he is lucky they send him money for school. Simeon remembers that he has never seen an Algerian with a Frenchwoman, although "African, West Indians or [Black] Americans [who] were students, artists, professionals [and] respectable" were often in the company of French people. Recalling the remark that he was a "white man," he tells Ahmed he would like to see the man who called him that. They go to the rooming house where Hossein lives. The place is "damp and filthy." In his room "there was no mattress or sheet on the narrow bed; a spare blanket, serving as a mattress, was stretched across the springs" (p. 91). Ahmed assures Simeon that the room" is only partly Hossein's. . . . He has it for eight hours a day. Two other men have it also for eight hours each. They sleep in rotation. That way, they split the rent three ways. None of them could afford to pay the rent alone" (p. 92).

Hossein tells Simeon that "Negroes in America should revolt, like we did." Suddenly, the police raid the building; Simeon shows his passport to the police inspector, who wants to know if he works for the FLN. "No," responds Simeon. "The inspector continued to study his face. 'You're a foreigner. I wouldn't advise you to get mixed up in our internal affairs; understand what I mean? You could be expelled from the country at the slightest suspicion. Understand?'" (p. 95) Simeon acknowledges and is now placed in the role of sympathizer with the Algerian cause. The other Afro-American expatriates do not involve themselves in the Algerians' plight. Rather, as Babe tells Simeon: "Algerians are white people. They feel like white people when they're with Negroes, don't make no mistake about it. A black man's got enough trouble in the world without going about defending white people" (p. 105). But Simeon remains unconvinced.

Several months have passed since Simeon's arrival. He meets Maria at the Le Tournon Café. Sitting there awaiting her, he wonders "how empty the lives of the expatriates could be." Maria arrives; she had been shopping. As she shows him and the nearby group the bracelet she just purchased, Ben Youssef, seated with

Hossein, casually tells her: "Probably some dirty Jew sold it to you." It is as though a bomb exploded. Maria is angry and says: "I am a dirty Jew." Youssef attempts to apologize, but Maria says, "No reason to be sorry. You said what you thought" (p. 123). Hossein, Simeon later discovers, hates Jews more than he hates the French. The frantic discussion ends as Hossein apologizes to her, Simeon, and others in the group.

Maria and Simeon discuss marriage. As he questions her, she becomes defensive. He tells her she is selfish, but she assures him she is not; rather, she cannot live in an "insane" world. Marriage plans begin slipping away.

As Simeon sits at the café the next day, he stares at a photograph in the newspaper; the photo show a group of Black children attempting to attend a school in a Southern American town. The children are guarded by soldiers who are holding off howling mobs. He is almost in tears as he recognizes the strength of conviction that the children in the photo pose and imagines the hell the children must be going through. His eyes rest on the face of a girl. He silently calls her "Lulu Belle," wondering: "Would Lulu Belle approve of him sitting way over here . . . drinking and passing the time away?" (p. 139). Babe Carter's vigorous "Never!" to returning to the States and his not wanting to be "integrated into the enemy" fill Simeon"s thoughts.

In early December, Joey the Drunk "drop[s] dead in the street." The day his body is placed on view, Simeon is also scheduled to attend a cocktail party with Maria. He goes first to the funeral parlor, then to the party; there he tells her he wants to leave. As they arrive at his apartment, Ahmed is waiting; he tells Simeon that Hossein has been arrested and tortured and is "being shipped to a concentration camp in Algeria." Ahmed is going to Algeria to join in the fight. Simeon is crushed by the news; they shake hands, and Ahmed departs.

"The Brother", Part Three, is the concluding section. Smith begins resolving the multipronged circumstances with Maria's eye operation; it is January and Simeon's eighth month abroad. The operation is a success, so they celebrate by taking a trip to Corsica, remaining there two full months. When the vacation ends, they return to Paris.

Maria is bursting with energy as she resumes her ambition to become a film actress. She continues working hard on a new play, appears on television, and attracts the attention of a producer, who promises her a small part in a future program. Simeon becomes jealous because she is often away. One day, suddenly, he proposes marriage. She tells him to "wait a while. . . . For the present I want to become a famous actress." Meanwhile, Babe and Marika are to be married, and Simeon is to be best man. The marriage takes place, but the wedding reception is marred by Doug's announcement that "Lumumba's dead. They killed him." (Patrice Lumumba was the Congolese premier in his troubled country.)

The Algerian War continues; Simeon is depressed by all the activities and reflects: "The foreigners—Simeon among them—lived in a fantasy world, like foam floating on the sea of

French society. They were not involved in current realities in France just as they were not involved in what was happening in their native countries" (p. 175). This statement by Simeon, via Smith, has far-reaching implications. In a not too subtle manner he indicts—factually?—the Third World expatriates, including himself, and the "romanticized" Black "colony." It also appears that The Stone Face, written after the unpublished "Ballets Roses/Pink Ballets," is a bitter indictment of French politics during the Algerian War and a direct attack on fellow expatriates more interested in pursuing their own "pleasures."

Smith explores the problems of the rest of the characters: Clyde becomes an alcoholic and womanizer; Jinx, his wife, has deserted him, taking their young daughter with her; Babe becomes a "homebody," quite content with his wife; and Benson has taken a Spanish mistress, drinks heavily, and berates the "United States in particular and the white world in general." Doug, meanwhile, shares his nights "between his American 'heiress' and the French girl he said he loved." He finally decides to marry the French girl. Harold appears to be the healthiest of the lot. He now lives in Vienna, visits Paris only on short trips, and is due to return to New York, the only place he "really feels at home." Although a Black man, Harold never heeds matters "of race or anytning else." Simeon's relationship with Maria continues fading. She has grown artistically, "headed for a very specific goal that did not include Simeon."

Ahmed returns to Paris; Simeon is elated to have his friend back in town and reflects on his own lack of growth during Ahmed's period in Algeria. At Ben Youssef's place for dinner Simeon meets two Algerian women who were tortured by the French. Ahmed details the horrible ordeal both women endured. Before leaving, Simeon is informed that curfew is being imposed on Algerians residing in Paris the following week; the Algerians plan to defy the edict. On a cold and damp day more than thirty thousand Algerians confront the police. Simeon witnesses old men beaten to the ground, some struck even after they were dead. "Along the Seine, police lifted unconscious Algerians from the ground and tossed them into the river"; among the dead is Ahmed, "his head battered to a pulp by police clubs." However, as Simeon watches the Algerians running madly, he notices a particular policeman's face: "It was Chris, Mike, their face. The policeman's face was distorted and twisted with joy of destruction, his eyes narrow, red dots of excitement on his deathly pale skin" (p. 203). Simeon's anger is at fever pitch as the faces of his earlier encounters with racism appear as one, superimposed on the policeman's face. He "did not think, but stumbled forward . . . and swung his fist into that hated face, with all his strength. Bone rang on bone; he saw the nose flatten and the blood spurt; and then he felt an excruciating pain in his head and the world blacked out." As he becomes conscious, he finds himself under arrest with scores of Algerians; he is released when it is discovered he is an American citizen.

In the two days following the riot and after being informed of Ahmed's death, the decision to leave Paris is his only thought. As he wrestles with possible places to go, he finds himself walking along the Champs Elysees. Suddenly Maria steps "out of a big American automobile, helped by a handsome and elegantly dressed man." She rushes to Simeon, talking rapidly; he feels awkward. She returns to her escort as Simeon walks to a ticket office to book passage to the United States. The Stone Face ends as he prepares to leave:

> On the eve of sailing, Simeon was surprised at his own calm. Shaving, he stared at his face in the mirror and realized with a shock how much he had aged. He walked into the living room, carrying the razor in his hand. Reaching into the closet, he took out the painting of the face and unrolled it. He did not need the image; the reality had penetrated. He slashed the canvas and threw the strips away (p. 212).

This ending, however, was not the original conclusion of the novel. William Gardner Smith originally had Simeon depart Paris for Africa.[97] An agreement with his publisher to revise the manuscript was based, in part, on actual racial events happening in America during the summer of 1963. Smith wrote: "If the Negro movement had reached this point before I wrote the book, "The Stone Face" would probably have had a different ending, with the hero returning to the States."[98] The publisher readily agreed to the change and, within two weeks, Smith wrote the revisions.[99]

Smith's maturity as a writer and his personal philosophy are evident in the book, as the novel also explored the expatriate scene in Paris. In effect, The Stone Face is Smith's "expatriate" novel, a genre that includes several Afro-American writers of the 1950s and 1960s.

While the reviews of the novel were mixed, most were favorable. Joseph Friedman, writing in the New York Times Book Review, commented: "The Stone Face" is a solid achievement. Among the most worthy young writers, Negro or white, count this one."[100] Freedomways critic Jean Carey Bond reviewed the novel in blistering terms, writing that "The Stone Face is not a very good novel. . . . The action is crudely contrived from beginning to end. . . . The novel has fleeting moments of technical originality. . . . Mr. Smith's values and thoughts are so well-formed that he may, in the future, be able to overcome his stylistic faults."[101] Nick Aaron Ford, commenting in Phylon, stated that the novel "establishes Smith as a serious contender for a place in the first rank of contemporary writers." He added, "On the whole, this is the best (not the most sensational) novel by a Negro writer since [Ralph] Ellison's Invisible Man. The quality of the experiences, the ironic overtones, the power of expression, and the refusal to court popularity by vulgarity of language make the reading of it a rewarding experience."[102]

From Paris to Africa 5

While William Gardner Smith continued living in Paris, the racial scene in America was becoming increasingly tense as Afro-Americans demanded racial equality in housing, employment, education, and so on. In August 1963 thousands of Blacks and some white liberals decended on the nation's capital in what was called the March on Washington. The date was August 28 when Dr. Martin Luther King, Jr., delivered a stunning speech, "I Have A Dream." Halfway around the world, in Accra, Ghana, another famous Black American, Dr. W. E. B. Du Bois, who had for more than sixty years championed the Black man's battle for liberation, died at the age of 95. The position Smith had taken for years earlier on the disenfranchisement of Blacks in America—one Du Bois had taken even before Smith's birth—had given both men equality in expatriate and exile status. Du Bois lived out his latter years in Africa, while Smith was still living in Europe with no intention of returning to his native soil, except for a brief visit. But his troubled thoughts would reflect on various things, as he wrote his sister Phyllis: "I sometimes feel guilty living way over here—especially when I read about "freedom marches" and the like. Maybe we'll come back eventually. But, sincerely, I can't stand that country [America]—not only racially, but also politically and culturally. I am for Castro and Mao Tse-tung! Ah, well! We'll drop the politics for the moment."[1]

Life was moving onward for the Smiths in the early autumn of 1963. He continued working at AFP while Solange was in the late stages of pregnancy. The immediate prospect of giving birth was anticipated with joy. The waiting period terminated when on October 4 their daughter, Michele, was born. Their three-room apartment on Avenue Gambetta was a place of happiness. "Bill was a very happy father. Bill always adored children. He was very proud of Michele and for a while he bored his friends stiff talking of nothing else."[2]

Near the end of the year, Mrs. Shirley Graham Du Bois, widow of Dr. W. E. B. Du Bois, arrived in Paris. Smith met with her and she "asked him to help start Ghanaian TV" in Accra, where she still resided.[3] He spoke to Solange about the offer, and they decided to go. They would have ample time to close out their affairs in Paris. Apart from what Mrs. Du Bois had said about Ghana, Smith knew little of the country. She described it thus in a magazine article published a few years later:

> The area of Ghana is approximately that of Great Britain, but the population is only seven and a half million. It was from the coast of Guinea, where Ghana is situated, that most of the slaves were carried off to America.
>
> In colonial days Accra was a sprawling commerical and administrative town, with a number of imposing, white Government buildings, one wide tree-lined street where large, comfortable houses set back in gardens. . . .
>
> Kwame Nkrumah returned to the Gold Coast in 1947 after an absence of fifteen years. . . . He had [gone] off to America [and had] managed to work his way through Lincoln University in Pennsylvania. After taking the master's degree, he went to London . . . and took courses at the London School of Economics. . . . Nkrumah returned home filled with ideas . . . to free his country from British rule! . . .
>
> In . . . 1949-51 . . . the newly organized Convention People's Party, under the leadership of Kwame Nkrumah, won the election. . . .
>
> Independence was celebrated March 6, 1957 when the name "Gold Coast" was discarded and the country took the name of an ancient West African kingdom—Ghana. The Republic of Ghana came into being July 1, 1960 and Kwame Nkrumah was inaugurated first President of the Republic.[4]

The new nation moved forward under its dynamic president. By 1963 the country seemed to be making progress, and the year ended with Nkrumah's addressing his nation as to the country's progress; foreign firms were requested to submit their books to government auditors. On January 1, 1964, the sixth attempt, dating back to the preindependence of Ghana, was made on Nkrumah's life.[5] Sixteen months earlier, on August 1, 1962, in a "bomb attack on . . . Nkrumah at Kulungugu . . . several innocent people lost their lives."[6]

This then would be the atmosphere—politics and foreign intrigue notwithstanding—of Ghana, the country William Gardner Smith and his family would arrive in several months hence. But Smith had known some of the politics of various African countries. In a letter to his mother he stated, "The Agence France Presse news agency . . . had planned to send me (at my request) to Kenya as a foreign correspondent last March [1963], but when we realized we were expecting a baby I called the trip off. (I would still like to go to Africa—I went to Ethiopia last May for the African Heads of State conference as a correspondent for the Agence.)"[7]

In mid-February 1964, responding to a letter sent him by his sister Phyllis, Smith wrote, "I am very happy. I have a marvelous wife, and a wonderful 4-month-old daughter. We live in a small, 3-room apartment which is not much by American standards, but we don't really care. My work for the French News Agency is very interesting: I am in charge of a desk (the Far East Desk), and though the salaries are low compared to the States, again I don't care."[8] Additionally, less than two months later, Solange wrote her mother-in-law that "Bill is the most attentive, admirable and loving father [and] he always wants to push the baby carriage himself when we take [our daughter] to the nearby park." She continued: "My mother . . . says she would like to meet you when she goes to the States to visit my grandfather on his 85th birthday. I don't know if Bill told you about this American branch of my family." She added, "My mother was born in Germany and came to France as a girl to escape Nazism. She married a Frenchman (my father) while the rest of the family emigrated to the States. . . . I have lots of relatives I have never met. . . .Anyway all this explains why my grandfather lives in Richmond [Virginia]. . . . He is a good man [and] keeps a picture of Michele and us hanging in his sitting room, his first great grandchild."[9]

But the long arm of American racism reached across the Atlantic to involve Smith physically. In early April, while attending a nightclub, he "broke his right shoulder [while fighting] a white American." On April 6 he was "being operated on right now (a bad break apparently) at the hospital." But the shoulder was not broken—it was a painful sprain—and he spent a few days at Hopital Cochin.[10]

Before spring had ended Smith was "invited to take part in a round table discussion . . . at the American Students' and Artists' Center in Paris concerning Paris 'Then'—in the twenties and thirties—and 'Now'—in the fifties and sixties.[11] The panel included "Virgil Thomson, leading American composer, for many years resident in Paris; Maria Jollas, leading lady of the 'thirities' literati, widow of Eugene Jollas, the founder of 'transition' magazine; Man Ray, painter and photographer closely associated with avant garde movements; John Levee, American painter, native of California; James Jones, noted American author; . . . William Gardner Smith, novelist; [and] the moderator: Janet Flanner, longtime Paris correspondent of The New Yorker."[12]

After introductory remarks by David Davis, Janet Flanner, a "Then" panelist, opened the discussion with three questions directed to the "Now" panelists: "I'd like to find why <u>your</u> generation has come over here, what satisfaction is given, <u>how</u> pleased are you with life here. What do you think, Mr. Painter, Mr. Levee." Levee responded, and the discussion was underway. The other panelists spoke before Smith finally got a chance to say something. After being interrupted without completing a sentence, he said,

> I think there is a difference between the "Thens" and us "Nows" in the sense that you had more positive reasons

for coming here, and we came here for mainly negative reasons. Let me put it this way. You talked about the ferment in Paris at the time, and I know there was the same sort of ferment in the States. It was the nineteen-twenties that had that ferment, and a relatively gay life, expensive life. You came to France, you found a cheaper life and you found a very vigorous artistic movement which, as you said, we are still living on. I think _we_ came for negative reasons. We came because we were pushed out, and I think you came because of a magnet that pulled you. Of course, I can give general reasons and specific reasons why I am in France. I can give standard ones, like I _do_ like that cliche of the sunset on the Seine, I _do_ like coming home late and seeing the light at five o'clock in the morning. And I like waving to the coal bargers when they pass the _Vert Galant_. I like the twisting streets. Gordon Heath, who's a singer here, says when he's asked why he stays in France instead of going back to the States, "I can't stand straight streets."

And I like the slowness. It's not really slow, but what I mean is I was delighted when I first came here and discovered that after a while, I didn't feel guilty anymore when I sat on a café terrace all afternoon. At first it was horrible. And I noticed that when Americans come over now and I say, "Sit down and have a drink," they sit down and after a half-hour they get nervous and they say shouldn't we go and see a museum or go someplace.

I had been offered a job just before I left the States with a magazine, for a lot of money. And I said, no, I'm going to France. The magazine editor came over here and he saw me living in a little room in a hotel with cold water and horrible flowered wallpaper, and he said, You turned down my job for _that_? And he didn't really understand when I said, "Yes, exactly for that."

Now specifically, two main things drove me out of the United States; negative things. I had been to Germany before. I went there in the occupation Army, and I was there a little over a year. When I got back to the States, I had the feeling of stifling. The two negative things were politics and race. McCarthy was around; I don't get along very well in that kind of atmosphere. My professor at Temple University, Professor Dunham, wrote a book, _Man Against Myth_. And he was called before the McCarthy committee and he said, when questioned, "I refuse to recognize your existence." Temple University fired him. I saw the ones who had suffered for just standing up and saying no, who didn't join any bandwagon, who wanted to think for themselves. Here in France—well, it's one of the freest countries in the world, but of course it has its paradoxical, dictatorial side too. French critics have all pointed out that neither _Doctor Strangelove_ or _Seven Days in May_ could have been made in France, it's not possible. And I

> talked to a French publisher about my last book; he told me it was very courageous to have written the book, but we can't publish it in France. It's peculiar: you can do things in the States, you can say things in the States, that you can't say in most other countries. And yet you feel so free in France, on an everyday level, just living here.
>
> Now about the racism. I had written three books, the third was an absolute move towards total silence. I discovered that I was not going to write anymore. My feeling was one of disgust and rage. When I wanted to go on vacation, I had to suddenly stop and look and say now wait a minute, am I accepted there? People can very easily say, well, let's go to Florida for a vacation. I have a lot of white friends and they can say it just like that. And when I say, now wait a minute, are you sure that's going to be all right, they look at me and say, what are you talking about, you're sensitive or something. And then we'd go and they would find out. It was constant irritations like this—and the daily headlines and so forth—which got me to the point psychologically where I just didn't want to write, because I didn't want to communicate. I didn't have anything else to say. To communicate means you like the other person, you want to explain something to the other person. That had been true with the first books when I had been younger.
>
> I had planned to come for a year, just like James [Jones]. That was twelve years ago.[13]

Meanwhile, a number of things had to be completed as the Smiths looked forward to their impending trip to Ghana. By the end of August they were ready to leave. Bidding farewell to friends, coworkers, neighbors, and acquaintances, they eagerly looked forward to Africa.

They arrived in Accra in early September 1964. After getting temporarily settled, Smith wrote to his mother:

> So here we are in Africa—and in the most dynamic and exciting African country, at that! We arrived a little over two weeks ago, and . . . I have a high post in a fascinating new field—television. I am now training journalists, and we shall begin our shows next spring. I got a really royal welcome when I arrived—four automobiles, including one with the director of television (the widow of the late Dr. W. E. B. Du Bois, who hired me in the first place)! President Nkrumah himself telephoned Mrs. Du Bois the night of our arrival to make sure we had gotten here all right. We are to go to the presidential palace to meet him soon, and Solange may teach him French!
>
> For a moment we are living in a big, lovely government house on the sea, opposite an old white

Danish castle. My foot rests on a lion-skin rug as I write! The weather is beautiful in this season—warm, with a strong breeze from the sea. . . . We have a private cook and a nurse to look after Michele! As soon as our regular house is repainted, we'll move into it. It is surrounded by a very big garden with trees—a small park, to tell the truth. . . .

We are very happy. All of us thrive in this eternal summer weather—especially Michele. Solange will probably work in the French section of the radio. For the first time in a long time I feel very useful! This country is going places—Nkrumah is a real African patriot, and he wants his country to develop fast. The people walk proud and tall—the women balancing baskets and other things on their heads, while carrying babies strapped to their backs. The city is not like a city at all—it is like a huge suburb, with most of the houses surrounded by big gardens and trees. There is a slum section—a hangover from colonialism—but it is being cleared up fast, and replaced by housing projects. My life and work make sense here; I am participating in something I approve of with all my heart. This is what I had always wanted, but had never quite found before.[14]

Among the first people Smith met were fellow Afro-Americans who were in Accra performing various functions as "heads of departments or near-heads of departments."[15] These Afro-Americans "were mostly pretty well-trained and educated people," a group of "young artists, writers, scholars, technologists, electronics people," numbering "maybe thirty."[16] While the total number of Afro-Americans in all of Ghana numbered approximately 120 during this period, those Black Americans in Accra could be called the "elites."[17] A quick rundown of the personnel in Ghana's capital city reads: writer and poet, Maya Angelou; artist, Tom Feelings; history and government professor, Dr. Martin Kilson; student, activist, and writer, Leslie Alexander Lacy; and writer and "Political Head of Afro-Americans" in Ghana, Julian Mayfield, among others.[18] Smith would get to know them marginally; in the meantime he was trying to absorb everything by sight, sound, and touch. Reflective, he later wrote,

First distant drums! I lay in bed, the windows open wide in vain against the heat of the night . . . and the sound of the drums came clearly on the wings of a furtive breeze. The drums played all night and I, the newly arrived, was fascinated. Several nights running I heard the drums and then, one night, drawn irresistibly, I got up, dressed, got in my car, and set off in the direction from which the sound seemed to be coming. . . . Driving along a road, the sky bright with stars and a moon lighting the thick trees on either side, I saw an old man standing in a doorway and

> asked: "Can you direct me to the drums? He said, "I'll take you there." We drove for half an hour and came to a big house in a clearing where, in a courtyard, dozens of persons were eating and laughing and dancing. . . . As we stood hesitant, an enormous jolly woman in flowing robes hailed us. "Come on in. Sit down. Dance." She . . . gently shoved us into chairs at a table and handed us plates piled high with fou-fou, an African starch smothered in delicious, very peppery stew. Icy bottles of beer found their way into our hands. Pretty young girls with colored kerchiefs around their heads insisted that we dance. . . . [N]ight birds screamed, and frogs croaked in the bush around. I stayed there until dawn. To this day, I still do not have the slightest idea where I was. . . . We were guests . . . brothers. That was normal. That was African.[19]

In November, two months after their arrival, Malcolm X—who had been in Accra during May—returned to Ghana after four months of visiting London and several African countries. Smith had never met Malcolm up to that point and did not recognize what his fellow expatriates noted in the troubled Malcolm. "Still, something was wrong when [he] came back to Ghana near the end of his journey. . . . It was all *different* this time, because Malcolm was different."[20] Smith, who had followed his growth in the early 1960's, knew about the break between the Muslims and Malcolm, a break that most envisioned as something to signal bodily harm to Malcolm. The seriousness of Malcolm's position and its implications drew the comment: "He looked very much like a fighter who had a bit of the wind taken out of him, who'd had a blow to the solar plexus."[21]

Malcolm's fear—although he disguised it thinly—emanated from the Muslims themselves. "He said there were Muslims [in America] who would [kill him] for Allah if somebody further up the [Muslim] hierarchy told them to."[22] Smith undoubtedly knew about the situation, and he, like others, "begged him to stay [in Accra]."[23] The group asked Malcolm to bring his family to Accra and "let that jazz [in America] cool off."[24] "But finally they had to put him on a plane. . . . Julian Mayfield watched him and thought: *He's got nowhere to go but back*."[25] In Smith and his wife, Malcolm inspired great admiration: "When we met him. . . Malcolm X was becoming a revolutionary. He was a great man to us."[26]

In the short span of four months after their arrival, the Smiths were witnesses to any number of changes; they were in a situation and environment they both enjoyed and were expecting another baby. The year would close with Smith reflecting on the dramatic change from a Paris setting to an African one. He recalled,

> I was swiftly struck by the visible signs of black sovereignty: the black ministers, heads of corporations, managers of big department stores, customs officials,

> bank clerks, salesmen, and the producers, directors, technicians, and journalists at the radio and television studios. The country appeared to be well organized. . . . The civil service was as efficient and also as bureaucratic as those encountered in other countries. . . . Unlike the situation in most other African countries, there were practically no beggars. A "workers' brigade" of road builders and farm workers had been created, partly to drain off any unemployed. "We are building a socialist society," Nkrumah said during my first meeting with him. "Socialism in an African context, socialism which takes African traditions into account."
>
> One thing I rapidly discovered was that the Black Power of Ghana, while much more real than in most African countries, had its grave limitations.[27]

Smith's official title was "Assistant Editor-in-Chief, Ghana Television." And, "very soon he was liked by everyone, and was working at the very highest levels."[28] While his principal activities were the setting up of the School of Journalism and lecturing at the ideological school at Winneba, he was also trying "to get off the ground a pet project of Nkrumah's and all other African journalists—an African News Agency."[29] An interesting observation of how Smith moved rapidly upward in the politics of Nkrumah's government was made by Julian Mayfield: "The President's office was like a Plantagenet court—full of intrigue and self-seeking—and a foreigner who had the ear of the President had to have mastered many political skills. I think Bill's secret was that he never seemed to want anything for himself (like a better job, thereby threatening someone else), and therefore everybody seemed to trust him and he got his way."[30] Totally immersed in his activities and motivated by his personal commitment to Ghana's growth, Smith remained on the go; he was extremely busy with his many duties, while his own writing suffered. The pleasant change in atmosphere in Ghana from the now cold, wintry weather in Paris had something to do with it. But to Smith, this was home—home without the racial, housing, and economic deprivation of white America. Here in Accra—as in Paris—he was treated as a man. Within a short time he adopted a new name, Kofi Abaka Smith.[31]

Abruptly, in the midst of the euphoric state he was now in--due to his happinesss with his assignments—a bulletin was passed to him: "Malcolm X had been assassinated!" Smith was stunned and instantly depressed.[32] Malcolm, as Smith was to find out, was killed by a hail of shotgun pellets and bullets at the Audubon Ballroom in New York City.[33] Ironically, Malcolm had written to Julian Mayfield that "if I'm killed . . . would you do what you can to see that some African government takes in Betty [Malcolm's wife] and the children?" The letter was sent to Mayfield in Ghana shortly before his death.[34]

Smith's political growth in Accra, meanwhile, was beginning to occur. By late spring he was promoted to "Director of the Institute of Journalism," although he "was asked by the government to keep . . . his [same] salary because of the financial crisis."[35] His plans to have his mother visit him and his family had to be altered. As he explained to his mother,

> Because of financial reasons and the coming of the second baby, we shall not be able to invite you here this year as we had hoped, and will have to postpone the trip for one year. . . . I had expected that my salary here would be higher than it is . . . and above all, I did not know how fantastically high the cost of living is here. . . . Now, with the coming of the baby in July, there are and will be further expenses.

In the letter he went on to say

> Solange is impatiently awaiting the arrival of our second child, who seems to be very energetic; and Michele is beginning to chatter away in a mixture of French, English and an African language.
>
> Incidentally, I have just returned to Accra after being sent to Paris on a brief official mission for the [Ghanaian] government. It was marvelous seeing Paris again, but I was glad to get back here. Life is calmer in Ghana, and it also has more purpose.
>
> I was supposed to go to Algiers at the end of June to attend the conference of Asian and African Heads of State, but I won't be able to do so because of the coming baby.[36]

On July 13 Solange gave birth to a son—to be named Claude—and Smith was delighted.

The government of Ghana continued having its economic troubles. The military, the middle class, and the police were constantly grumbling about Nkrumah's politics and the country's only political party, the Convention People's Party (CPP). Smith would hear of the dissatisfaction from different people, primarily members of the officer's corps of the army. "Nkrumah was accused of becoming increasingly repressive, and while the stories [were] exaggerated, it is true that [in 1963] security measures were strengthened where the President's person was concerned."[37]

Prior to Smith's arrival in the country and during the first months of his stay

> charges of a pro-Russian and pro-Chinese "shift" and of extravagant expenditure became more frequent. Yet Nkrumah tried to maintain good relations with the United States, as with the other Western powers. Kaiser [Aluminum Company] was rushing the work on the Volta River Dam; Peace Corps teachers and geologists were welcomed into the country. But the CPP was also trying to set up state farms and state-owned factories, much to the disgust of U.S. economic advisers who dubbed these enterprises inefficient and who now

> suggested that the Seven Year Development Plan was in any case too ambitious. American policy had changed. Economists had one standard prescription: economy. Nkrumah would stubbornly answer back: development. By 1964 he was forced to borrow at very high rates of interest to finance projects considered vital to the plan, and the clamor grew that he was wasting the country's monetary reserves. *Newsweek* is honest enough, however, to introduce a more basic factor in Ghana's economic difficulties, even while endorsing the charge of waste: "lavish spending on show-case projects, together with a sharp drop in the world price of cocoa, brought once thriving Ghana to the brink of bankrupcy.[38]

But it appeared that Nkrumah's government was already in deep trouble. "Another painful discovery was of the almost universal corruption in high places. Ministers and high officials were using their posts to promote private businesses; they were hiring relatives or fellow tribesmen at high salaries; many of them were salting money away in foreign banks."[39] Smith, acknowledging dismally to himself what was going on, would later add, "One of the most difficult things to live with was the shocking social inequality, which was apparently a legacy of the country's colonial past. You either lived well or you lived very poorly, indeed. You lived in a big, comfortable house with servants, or, with rare exceptions, you lived in a shack without electricity, gas or toilet facilities, cooking your meals on a wood fire outside the house."[40]

As things kept moving downward for the Nkrumah government, Smith kept up his correspondence with his relatives in Philadelphia, never indicating the true picture of events developing in Ghana. In an earlier letter to his mother he requested that she come to Ghana on a visit to meet Solange and the children. In a response to the letter from his sister Phyllis, asking if she could come along with their mother, Smith wrote

> of course you can come to Ghana with Mom! . . . I'm delighted at the idea. Solange and I are trying like mad now to save the money for Mom's air trip.
>
> It's only when you *leave* the United States that your real education can *begin*. You mention what you call my bitterness. . . . First of all, bitterness is not quite the word—I just don't like the United States: I don't like its racism, I don't like its Puritanical hypocrisy, I don't like its commercialism, I don't like its spiritual emptiness and I don't like its foreign policy . . . and I have no intention of ever living there again. I'll probably stay in Africa: I feel at home here.[41]

But Smith's—and Ghana's—situation was actually undergoing severe changes.

He could not, at this point, see or even envision what would happen in Accra in the following months. Increased dissatisfaction was steadily building among the top levels of the Ghanaian military, its solid middle class, and the general populace. The Vietnam War had reached a point at which Nkrumah flew from Accra to Hanoi on February 21 to accept President Ho Chi Minh's second invitation to him for "talks."[42] He "informed Peking, Moscow and Washington of his intentions,"[43] but as he prepared to depart for Hanoi, "it [was] alleged that the U.S. Ambassador, Franklin Williams, offered . . . 13 million dollars to carry out a coup d'état . . . if they would assassinate [Nkrumah] at Accra Airport as [he] prepared to leave for Hanoi."[44]

The planned attempt never materialized, because the designated assassin is alleged to have said, "I think I will fail," and declined the offer. So apparently did the others."[45] Seventy-two hours later, February 24, an early morning radio announcement was made in Accra: "The Armed Forces of Ghana, together with the Police, have taken over the Government of Ghana. Remain calm and stay inside your homes. Long live Ghana."[46]

The coup began at approximately 4:30 a.m. Smith, Solange, and the children were asleep at that hour. Cannon and machine-gun fire awakened Solange. She listened for a short while and thought the nearby army camp was on maneuvers. She awakened Smith, who was sleeping through the noise, with the distinct feeling something was wrong. He listened, said nothing, and returned to sleep. As the various guns continued to belch out noises, he abruptly came wide awake. He realized that something was definitely out of order. Dressing rapidly, he rushed to his car and drove to the institute to meet with now frightened students. Speaking—almost ordering—in a harsh voice, he said the rebels should be stopped. Desperate moments ticked away, Smith wondering almost aloud how a thing like this could happen. Suddenly, six men carrying machine guns appeared; he was taken to a now rebel-controlled police station.

Solange, meanwhile, fearing for her children, herself, and her husband, held Michele and Claude close to her at home for the rest of the day. Was Bill all right? There was no way to be sure.[47]

Smith returned home late in the day to a terribly frightened family. After trying to calm and soothe them, he told his wife what had happened: He had been arrested, interrogated, and released with the order, "Leave Ghana immediately!" Since they normally lived with not too many bulky items, their few household items did not constitute a major moving operation. Gathering bits and pieces to take with them, they were ready to leave in the next few days. While they were en route to the airport—ten days after the coup—guards, soldiers, police officers, armed civilians, and several bold Ghanaians stopped their car several times, inquiring briskly—of all things—if the car had been paid for in full![48]

They arrived at the airport unharmed and departed for Geneva,

Switzerland.[49] William Gardner Smith's trip to Ghana—his second country of expatriation—had lasted less than a year and a half.

Return to Paris and America 6

Back in Europe again, the Smiths immediately went to the home of Solange's parents in Megève, France. After settling down, less than a month after the coup, Smith wrote to his mother:

> We are now safely out of Ghana, and resting for a few days at the home of Solange's parents in Megève. In a few days, we shall return to Paris. Luckily, I have received a letter from Agence France-Presse, stating that they would like me to return to work with them; otherwise, we would have been in financial trouble.
>
> I am very sad to have had to leave Ghana—especially since we had been looking forward to your visit and to the prospect of showing you and Phyllis around. I had been extremely active: directing the Institute of Journalism, lecturing on world politics at Winneba Institute, writing for radio and being a member of a number of the President's committees. In addition, I had been on the verge of bringing out a new magazine, a sort of African version of "Time."
>
> I want to return to Africa eventually. But for the moment, I must reestablish my family here. Incidentally, did I tell you that the new regime in Ghana, after arresting me and ordering me to leave the country, finally offered me a job?[1] They sent an emissary to tell me that if I "cooperated," I could be Editor-in-Chief of a new magazine. I refused to work for them [and] decided to return to France.
>
> When will we see each other again? The absence has endured too long, now—we'll find it increasingly difficult to know each other when we meet. But the financial problem is enormous; and so is the political problem, since there is always the chance that the U.S. Government will take my passport if I return for a visit. At any rate, the problem must be solved, and I am thinking of ways perhaps I can be sent on assignment to

> the U.S. by the Agence, eventually. I want to see all of you; I want to recover my link with the family and the past. I love all of you.[1]

Smith and his family spent almost a month resting and recovering from the psychological strains of the situation in Ghana. Before returning to Paris and resuming his work at AFP, he wrote to his sister Phyllis:

> A brief, sad note about your postponed trip! I had looked forward to receiving you and Mom. I wanted to show you the new, dynamic Africa—I am sure you would have been very pleasantly surprised. But the American C.I.A. and the Ghananian upper class—represented by the army—moved too quickly.
>
> The coup itself was no surprise to me, since I knew many officers [and] knew their sentiments. It was only the timing, and the relative ease of the success, which were unexpected. At any rate, the American and British are now back in the saddle again—temporarily.
>
> I am really sad that we shall not be able to meet in Ghana. . . . As the years pass, despite the distance, I feel I somehow draw closer [and] closer to my family—my roots. . . .[2]

The Smiths arrived in Paris and found an apartment to their liking on rue Geoffroy St. Hilaire, a comfortable two-room place, "facing one of the largest and nicest public gardens [Jardin des Plantes] in Paris."[3] He was back at Agence France-Presse and, claimed to Solange in a letter to his mother, "they were only too happy to [have] him back, [as] he is the best journalist on his desk!"[4] Although "it was a bit difficult for [them] to adjust at first, especially for Bill," things eventually fell into place.[5] The year had been a very trying time for the family.[6]

Back at AFP as a senior editor, Smith welcomed renewing friendships with people he had not seen in over a year and a half. Too, he began writing again. The image of Ghana was still very clear in his mind, and he started outlining a nonfiction manuscript about what he had lived through in Ghana. Just before the year ended, he sent the outline to his publishers, who read it and responded without committing themselves. Smith then wrote them, "I fully understand that you are still 'a bit nervous' about signing a contract on the basis of an outline; I, too, am a bit nervous, since I have launched into the kind of book I had never attempted before." He went on, "Things are going well for me. . . . I have just been named editor-in-chief of the English language service (Far East, North America, Scandinavia and Britain) of Agence France-Presse. Its a new challenge, and I'm quite excited about it."[7]

On Saturday, July 29, 1967, Smith's mother received a Western Union telegram that simply stated: "ARRIVING TO COVER EVENTS SEE YOU SOON LOVE BILL."[8] The telegram had been routed from

Paris, and his mother immediately told the members of the family and several neighbors the good news. AFP was sending him to the United States to cover the riots in America. In Philadelphia, as well as other American communities, various factions in the Black areas were burning, looting, and killing; the world at large was watching via television footage, radio, and newspaper accounts of the action. AFP had made a decision to cover the situation with its own representative.

Whatever thoughts ran through Smith's mind once the decision was reached can only be assumed. It would be fair to say, however, that he must have been tense. By now he was several months past the age of forty. When he had left America, he was going on twenty-five. He had put on weight over the years; maturing had served him well. And, deep down inside, he very much wanted to see his mother and the rest of the family. While it is not clear whether he arrived in Chicago or New York, in a short time he was in Philadelphia. En route to his parents' home, he was undoubtedly overwhelmed by the changes that had taken place since 1951. The numerous new buildings, the declining state of his favorite street—South Street—and the changes in the political structure had to make an impression on him.

He spent the first days in South Philadelphia, trying to assess his feelings after his long absence. Eventually he would see as many relatives and friends as possible, including his former wife, Mary. His sister Phyllis was at Wesleyan University in Connecticut taking graduate courses and would return to Philadelphia before the end of summer. His brother, Douglas, was still in the Navy and could not get home.[9] The whirlwind days and nights included stopping at his former place of employment, the Pittsburgh Courier bureau on Broad Street. Later he met with his longtime friend Darryl Gordon, with whom he wanted to talk about the changes in the city and America during his almost sixteen years as an expatriate.[10]

The time at home passed quickly, and since his return was based on the assignment for AFP, it was time to crisscross the country in what would be a series of interviews with Blacks and whites in various walks of life. Less than a week after returning to the states he started westward, formally, as a correspondent.

The almost four weeks of investigative reporting on Black conditions leading to the 1967 uprising took him to Cleveland, New York, Detriot, Brooklyn, Chicago, Washington, D.C., San Francisco, and Los Angeles, as well as his native city of Philadelphia. The nationwide firsthand reporting for AFP ended when he returned to South Philadelphia on Friday, September 1. Phyllis had returned from Connecticut and finally met her brother the day he reappeared at their parents' home. The tearful reunion was one of joy; later that evening he took Phyllis and Mary to dinner.[11]

The next day he began packing for the return trip to Paris. Tired but satisfied with the many interviews he had conducted, he checked the airlines office for flight time. Later in the day he left South Philadelphia for Kennedy Airport in New York.

After sixteen years away from the United States, Philadelphia, family, relatives, and friends, Smith probably reflected that he had spent only a total of six days with his family and friends.[12]

William Gardner Smith returned to Paris on September 3, 1967, after having spent approximately a month as a correspondent in the US. He reflected on his return in a letter to his mother:

> It was marvelous seeing you again, and my only regret is that my trip had to be cut short. Of course, I was happy to get back to my wife and children again; but, after 16 years of absence, I finally spent very little time—six days in all—in Philadelphia. But I am happy at the prospect that it will happen again undoubtedly next year—and, if I am to believe the people at our New York office, maybe even earlier.
>
> The visit was extremely important for me psychologically. It reattached me strongly to my roots—to you and the rest of the family. All of you, and particularly "the kids" who were small when I left, have taken on greater "reality" for me. After the first day, it seemed absolutely natural—like "old times"—to sit in the kitchen and eat scrapple and eggs. It was as though I had never been away. I was delighted to find all of you in such high spirits and good health. I am sorry I did not see Doug [Smith's half brother], but it was good to talk to him by phone.

He went on to say, explaining the abruptness of his departure, due to the television appearance he was committed to in Paris, that

> Today is Saturday, and I arrived last Sunday night. Solange and the kids were at the airport, in her brother's car, to pick me up. . . . I did the television program last Tuesday, but have not yet gone back to work at the News Agency (I go back on Monday). I am not sure I have quite "readjusted" to Paris yet. The trip to the States made such an impact on me, and seeing you and old friends was so wonderful and startling, that I am still under their effect. I see Paris and everything else through different eyes.
>
> Doug [Smith's stepfather] was in good form. In fact, everybody seemed in excellent spirits. I felt all warm and grateful at the welcome I got from everybody.[13]

Smith's return to Paris with the observations he had made in the United States from "Maine to California examining riot situations and their potential" kept him on the go after arriving on September 3.[14] He wrote Mary,

> Since my return, I have been speaking on an endless round of television and radio programs, and public

> meetings. Everybody wants to know what's going on in the States, and I have suddenly been raised to the rank of Europe's No. 1 expert on the question. It's exhilarating and tiring.
>
> It was a relief to get back to Paris, despite my regret at leaving the U.S.—particularly, Philadelphia—earlier than expected. Life seems so much more human and relaxed here, and there are no racial tensions. My family is well, and they had all missed me. . . .
>
> I really enjoy my job: it combines creativity with a sense of liberty. It is nice to know that, bit by bit, I shall undoubtedly travel all over the world, gathering material which can eventually serve in books. I doubt that I shall ever live in the States again, though some Black Nationalists keep pressing me to do so.[15]

His hectic pace continued for several additional weeks with a "three-week trip to Algiers, to cover a conference of 77 countries (African, Asian and Latin American) on economic problems" that began on October 6.[16] Tired, he returned to Paris to a well-deserved rest. By now the outline for his prospective nonfiction book had grown, and he had given it the title "Through Dark Eyes."[17] A close friend of his wrote to Smith's publishers, "I think he is going to write a fine book; I shall see some pages of it in a fortnight. He is quite a prominent journalist now, as you know (head of AFP's English language service) and I personally have always felt that his novels reveal a journalist's talent. . . . This could be the book on the subject." The brief letter ended on an interesting note: "[Smith] is, by the way, Stokely Carmichael's main contact in Paris, so there really isn't any danger of black back-lash against him."[18]

On March 23, 1968, Smith's stepfather died of a heart attack. Smith was notified by his mother and he "was torn between two choices: either to fly home for the funeral, or send money to my mother—I did not have enough for both. I finally decided on the latter. As a child, I did not like Doug, but we came closer together as I got older, and my contact with him was really good when I was there last year."[19]

Two years earlier Smith had reflected on his experiences in Africa for a possible book. But the trip to America eight months earlier was fresh in his mind, and he decided to write down his impressions, putting the projected book on his African experiences to one side. He commented later that "I can show how things look through the eyes of someone who returns [to America] after a long absence."[20]

Two weeks subsequent to his stepfather's death there had occurred the death of a person known on the international level. Dr. Martin Luther King, Jr., a champion of nonviolence, died in Memphis, Tennessee, assassinated in an act so despicable that Smith wrote to Mary:

> I was within a hair's breadth of returning to the U.S. last weekend, after Dr. King's murder. At 2 a.m. on the Saturday after the slaying, when disorders were spreading throughout the country, I received a telephone call from the Editor-in-Chief asking whether my "passport is up to date." I was scheduled to leave the following Monday; but by then things seemed to have calmed down considerably, and my trip was called off.
>
> The murder of Dr. King shocked me, even though it did not surprise me—nothing surprises me over there.[21]

Meanwhile, martial troubles had begun between Solange and Smith; their marriage was slowly disintegrating. For extremely personal reasons the relationship could not be reconciled, and within the next few months the marriage would be reduced to a separation. By early fall of 1968 Smith had moved into a hotel, but continued seeing his children at least twice a week.

A friend of Smith remembers that he invited him to dinner at his home not long after the separation:

> Bill asked if he could bring his fiancee, an Indian girl. Then my wife began to worry about what this would do to her menu, for if the young woman was a Hindu she wouldn't touch meat. My wife thought she'd resolve the issue by filling a variety of bowls with salads and vegetables. At the dinner table I told Ira about our perplexity, and said that I hoped we had done the right thing. She replied, her limpid dark eyes looking squarely at me: "But I'm Jewish."
>
> Ira's entrance was the sensation of that evening. She was a tall, slender girl with finely chiseled features, a light-brown complextion, a swan's neck and a swan's grace. She wore a stunning, finely textured silk sari and open sandals; on her forehead she had put a tiny spot of reddish powder called a tika, originally a Hindu symbol, now used as a kind of makeup, like lipstick.
>
> Speaking a precise and beautiful English with a slight British accent, she told me that her father's father had been Chief Judicial Officer of Junagad [a town in India]. Her father [had] been a judge on the High Court of Patna [and] when he retired in 1952 he was Chief Justice of that Court.[22]

Ira Reuben had arrived in Paris in late November 1967 from London to work at the Indian Embassy and learn to speak French.[23] Within her first year in Paris she had met Smith; in autumn of the following year they fell in love and began living together. Fifteen years younger than Smith, Ira had been born in 1942 in Ranchi, India.[23]

Meanwhile, Solange and Smith had filed for a formal separation. He continued writing about his experiences in America, a project that he had begun in late 1967. Ira and Smith would, from time to time, go to the movies or just talk;

at other times they would walk around Paris, strolling in sections seldom visited by tourists. The months continued to roll by as he continued at least once a week to visit his children, who were living with their mother.

During the early months of 1969, the new book was rapidly reaching the final stages; simultaneously, the separation of Smith and Solange neared divorce. By now he and Ira had moved from a hotel room to a small apartment on rue du Roi de Sicile. In early 1970 the marriage between Smith and Solange was legally terminated. But, as Solange explains,

> Bill and I were a very tender couple. Many of our ideas were similar. On one point we were very different: love was not as much for me the central focus of his life. He used to say: "I cannot find in a single person everything I am looking for. What I want is the whole world." Bill was always available for another "experience." There was no limitation to his desires. He "preferred" me and never thought of getting a divorce. . . . He adores his children. The divorce was very hard for both of us. . . We were both sorry to hurt each other, we cried like two idiots, there was never a word of hatred or even anger when we divorced. We always respected each other and the children were not torn between us two. We had the same lawyer. Bill volunteered to give the children a pension. . . . I left it free for him to visit the children or have them with him whenever he chose. So he visited them twice a week, and had them at his home every weekend.[25]

On Saturday, July 4, 1970, several months after the divorce, Ira and Bill married. The newlyweds had another joy, for the new book Smith had been working on was now published. The title of the book, based on his trip to the United States almost three years earlier, was <u>Return to Black America</u>.

<u>Return to Black America</u>, Smith's fifth published book, is a nonfiction work that explores, in part, his 1967 trip to the US.[26] Part One of the two-part book is entitled "Three Continents" and includes a section called "America: Initial Impressions," which is further divided into seven subsections. The subjects are personal to Smith and are dealt with in a clear and precise language that serves to introduce the reader to the background of the author and his travels around America, where he returned after an absence of approximately sixteen years. He reflects, on the opening page, that he had spent "well over a third of [his] life" outside of the United States, mainly in Paris.

In "Homecoming" Smith writes too briefly about his family; the reader expects more reaction to and from family members on his extended stay in Europe. He spends approximately three pages detailing only highlights of his family's poor background, with the notable exception of his "great-uncle, Charles Gilpin . . . one of the greatest actors in the country; Eugene O'Neill wrote

The Emperor Jones for him." He does not mention his wife or children in Paris; in effect, the reader knows very little about William Gardner Smith or his personal thoughts or feelings. "Family Reunion" serves as the start of his quest for examining the changes in his old neighborhood; moreover, it places the book in the arena of politics. Return to Black America is really Smith's probing worldwide politics as he encountered them and his reflections upon them.

Section II, "Black Man in Europe," consists of three subsections. It begins with a thirteen-page subsection in which Smith gives an insight into the best-known expatriates in Paris in the post-World War II years. At one point he details the "race" conversation the men are having; most agree that they are never returning to America, the lone exception being writer James Baldwin. He says, "There's a question of roots. Particularly for an artist. One has to return to one's roots, whatever and wherever they are, to be nourished and to grow. . . . But one has to go back. One has to go back to one's roots." Fellow writer Chester Himes is unimpressed and asks him, "What roots? You go back if you like." Agreeing with Himes, writer Richard Wright, in Paris since 1947, "said in his heavy Mississippi accent, 'All right, be a glutton for punishment. Not me. The U.S. has seen the last of me'" (p. 62). Smith said that most of the expartiates were escaping the "race problem," seeking, in effect, "a racial Shangri-la"; in Paris they were "free men," although there was a price to be paid, as most of them found it hard "to live at peace with himself." He wrote of the typical expatriate, in an almost self-confessional tone, that "He paid it in a painful tearing of himself from his past . . . from which he would never escape despite the miles or the decades separating him [from the US]. . . . He paid for it . . . in a sort of rootlessness. . . . The black man, no matter how long he lived in Europe, drifted through those societies an eternal 'foreigner' among eternal strangers" (p. 71). The statement is more of a personal insight into Smith's many years as an expatriate than he allowed himself in any of his previous writings or public pronouncements.

The concluding section, "The Call of Africa," covers Smith's trip to Ghana. He begins with "Dream and Reality," moves on to "The Question of Race," and ends the trio of subsections with "The Black Mystique and the Fall of Nkrumah." In "The Question of Race" he touches on a very sensitive subject: the differences between Afro-Americans, West Indians, and Africans. During the last year he lived in Ghana, Smith met a young Afro-American man who was completely disillusioned with Ghanaians. The unnamed young man assumed the phrase "We are black, therefore we are brothers" meant something to the Africans. Smith's assessment of the disillusioned man's "nationalism"

> is incomprehensible in tribal societies where the hereditary enemies have, precisely, been black. . . . In Liberia, we have a peculiar and unpleasant situation in which a black minority that emigrated from the United States has now established a caste-like control over the

> native population. . . . The Africans know this, and therefore they cannot consider that the words "blackness" and "brotherhood" are necessarily synonymous (pp. 102-3).

But Smith is quick to add that the African realizes "that white racism exists" and that the "political importance" of race in the diaspora is beginning to be understood. The sixteen pages that make up this subsection focus on Accra and give an insight into Ghana's revolution in 1966; they also serve as a prelude to the remaining portion of the book, in which Smith continues his observations and thoughts on politics and various people in the United States.

Part Two, "The American Jigsaw," also in three subsections, brings the book to its high point as Smith writes of travels to a number of cities in his native land. He conducts in-depth interviews with members of the black middle class and those of lesser status. "Variations on a Theme" constitutes the first section; "The White Involvement" is the heading of the second; and "Towards the Future" completes the seventy-two pages of Part Two. The reading is extremely informative because of Smith's candid views and comments on the United States as witnessed by the longtime expatriate.

In "The Black Debate" he sums up his political observations made in Algeria and Ghana, drawing on the politics of France in relationship to Algeria. In particular, he sees a striking similarity between the FLN (National Liberation Front of Algeria) and the Black Power movement and advocates in America. He poses a number of questions as to what tactics should be employed politically and economically; he poses the questions without attempting to answer them.

Rap Brown, chairman of SNCC, is the subject of "A Young Turk." This seven-page interview gives a critical insight into Brown's position in 1967 America. In "A Softer Tone" two of Smith's cousins are described as "less radical" in the everchanging Black communities. Apparently content with their positions—they work for the government as secretaries; their husbands are also employed by the government—they pose two contradictions that Smith encountered in his nationwide travels. Actor and writer Julian Mayfield, living in Washington, D.C., whom Smith had met in Ghana, introduces him to a black schoolteacher; the teacher informs Smith that "there is a sort of Negro middle-class here . . . and they don't feel very revolutionary." In Cleveland the conservative NAACP identifies Ahmed Evans as the local troublemaker; Smith meets Evans, who is, indeed, a "revolutionary." Evans believes that one of the main reasons for the inability of Black people to unite is that the Black middle class "don't want to do nothing to help their Black brothers" (p. 128). Smith continues moving across America, Detroit, San Francisco, Los Angeles, and then back to the East Coast. In his travels he meets Carl Loeb, James Boggs, Nadine Brown, Reverend Albert B. Cleague, French writer Pierre Loiseaux, and Elijah Muhammad, among a cross-section of people either involved in "revolutionary activities" or opposed to change.

In a later subsection Smith describes meeting Max, a returned expatriate, in Los Angeles. The men had known each other for more than ten years in Paris. Max is an Irish-American, a former Marine Corps officer during World War II. Max's return to America is the subject of "Talk with a Future Birchite," the third subsection of "The White Involvement." Invited to Max's apartment, they talk briefly of Paris and "those bulls in Pamplona." Their conversation turns abruptly as Max says: "I suppose the views of a conservative honky wouldn't interest you." Smith says it would. Max then says, "You always were open-minded. It's a pity, it's a pity that . . . Well, to put it stupidly, that you're not . . . white. . . . I just wanted to say that you're one of the Negroes I always respected." Smith takes the statement in stride, letting Max further qualify his latent racist theories. From time to time Smith injects a question, letting Max expound on his impossible set of "facts." After a period of Max's rambling details, Smith tells him: I can't see what the equality or inequality of individuals has to do with <u>race</u>." Max replies,

> "No. I agree. Believe it or not, I'm sorry about the situation; I know it's unjust. But it's an historical accident, it happens to exist. . . . There's no real solution unless we ship all the Negroes back to Africa. That's not very realistic. So, in the given circumstances, as [William] Faulkner more or less said, when the black-white showdown comes, I'll be on the streets on the side of the whites. I'm sorry. I hope I don't see you on the other side of the barricade. I'd have to shoot you" (p. 165).

Smith's taking the pulse of America after his sixteen year expatriation is almost personified by Max's statement.

"Towards the Future" is the concluding section of <u>Return to Black America</u>. Smith reviews "Black America and the World," touching upon a Black Power committee set up in Paris, General Charles de Gaulle's intervening personally to allow Stokely Carmichael "permission to enter France and remain for as long as he wished," Smith's trip to Algiers in September 1968, and his meetings with "Castro-style revolutionaries from Latin America and radical students in Europe."

In "A Black Liberation Front?" he examines the frustrations of Black militants wanting to create a "Black Liberation Front" and being thwarted by, they felt, the Citizen's Action Committee in Detroit and the Black Power Conference in Newark.

"Society in Crisis" is the closing subsection. Smith sums up his position to the solution of the "black problem" in eleven words: <u>"only by a radical transformation of the surrounding white society itself."</u> He reminds the reader that Malcolm X, Martin Luther King, John F. Kennedy, and Robert Kennedy have been assassinated and that "the American crime rate is the highest in the world. It is a country of 'rugged individualism' [and] institutionalized racism." Smith ends <u>Return to Black America</u> on a bitter note: "Ours is a country born in violence, bred in violence: a glorifier of violence. So, it looks as though we're in for a long, hot decade or two."

A couple of minor inaccuracies hardly mar this very readable book. For instance, Smith states that he returned to the United States in the summer of 1967 and again during the summer of 1968 (p. 4). There is, however, no proof that he returned to America in 1968 as a correspondent for AFP, for French radio, or in any capacity. "The Black Panthers, a minor group when I went back to the U.S. in 1957" (p. 157), should read "in 1967," but this is obviously a typographical error.

Return to Black America received a variety of reviews. O. A. Bouise, critic for Book Sellers, enjoyed Smith's nonfiction book, stating, "I recommend this book, both for the effective detailing of the current climate of Black American thinking and for spelling out the summary meaning which these details imply."[27] The New Yorker went on to say the book, "turns out to be a very valuable piece of work. . . . Mr. Smith . . . appraises the Black-Power movement in the United States. . . . What we get here is a view, from an almost unique vantage point, a movement that intends to, and could, transform our whole society, written with sympathy for the people most concerned but with an intelligent skepticism about the more extravagant notions that are currently in the air."[28]

Smith later described Return to Black America as "a dismal failure, due . . . mainly to the publisher's lack of interest."[29] Another possible source of his irritation could have been the fact that in the section reserved for "other books by" the author, his fourth novel is listed as "The Stone Age" and his previous books are listed out of sequence.

In 1972 Return to Black America was translated and reprinted in French.[30]

Do Not Go Gentle into that Good Night 7

Two months after their marriage Ira became pregnant, but Smith continued to see his other children, mostly on weekends.

The year 1971 was just underway when he received a letter from Jerry Bryant, a professor of English at California State College at Haywood. The letter had an article about Smith attached, written by Bryant. He answered the letter, stating

> It is a pity that not all my novels have been published; in fact, the two best novels I have ever written, in my opinion, were refused by the publishers, on the grounds that they would not sell. I have lost the manuscript of one, and the first hundred pages of the manuscript of the other. . . . One of these books—the one of which I still have the major part of the manuscript—deals with a black politician who rises quite high on the American political scene, but who is destroyed because he ignores his ghetto origins.
>
> The fact is that I never consciously arrived at a generalization of my own themes—I simply wrote books, out of the emotions that haunted me. . . .
>
> However, there is an anecdote which could interest you. Originally, as I wrote the book, the hero of *The Stone Face* did not, at the end, return to the U.S.—he went to Africa. After I had delivered the manuscript to Farrar, Straus, some big racial movement occurred in the States—I think the March on Washington—and I wrote to the publisher that, were I concluding the book at that moment, I would send the hero back to the U.S. I got an immediate, urgent letter suggesting that I make that change. . . .
>
> I must say that, while I have published five books, I have actually written ten—all manuscripts lost in travel, except part of the one I mentioned to you. I can now put my finger on one of the reasons why: As my books shifted from "communication" to the unaggressive

> affirmation of our own worth, I think they became less accessible to white readers (or at least white publishers). ("Remember that you are writing for the white middle class, which can afford to pay six dollars for a book," a publisher once told me.)[1]

Smith continued working on his new book and remained at AFP. In late May, Ira gave birth to a daughter; the baby was named Rachel. During the summer he joined the older children at Solange's mother and stepfather's home at Megève; this trip was, by now, an annual occasion. Smith did, however, return to America in November. While his arrival was in Miami on a flight from South America, where he visited and with whom remain a mystery. Moreover, his departure date back to Paris is unknown.[2]

In early July 1972 he received a letter from his mother. He responded:

> We had thought that you must have been disgusted with your son for having divorced (again) and remarried. . . . The divorce was by mutual consent, and we remain good friends. [Solange] and Ira get on well. I go to see Michele and Claude at Solange's place, and the kids all stay here weekends.
>
> We have moved: the old, two-room apartment was not big enough to accommodate the new family plus Claude and Michele on weekends. . . . Rachel, in the meantime, is delighted because she can run from room to room to her heart's content.
>
> Ira . . . is a marvelous mother, one who really loves children and is happiest with them. I had not really intended having a third child, but once I remarried this became inevitable, and now I am pleased. . . .
>
> Solange's mother and step-father still treat me like a son-in-law, to everyone's astonishment. But the fact that we all retain this natural friendship has had a marvelous effect on Solange's two children. . . .
>
> I am well, with the grey hairs increasing. When I returned from the States in 1967 I was surprised that I had become, through my articles, quite a celebrity, the number one expert on what was happening in Black America! I was always on radio, television, etc., my articles were published around the world, and I was even invited to Switzerland to speak.
>
> I am the editor-in-chief of the English Service of Agence France-Presse, and am also becoming something of a world traveller as special correspondent for the agency. I went to Belgrade for the non-aligned conference, to Morocco for the Arab summit conference, and my last voyage was to Peru last October for an important economic conference. Health-wise I am all right, except that I have high-blood presure and attacks of gout![3]

With summer over and the vacation with Michele and Claude

well spent—including more writing on the new book—Smith returned to work at AFP. In October he received a letter from Jerry Bryant, who was teaching at the University of Copenhagen for the college year 1972-73, saying that he and his wife were to visit Paris. Once in Paris, Bryant and Smith "met twice, once at [Smith's] favorite Chinese restaurant, and once at [Smith's] apartment."[4] As Bryant remembers, Smith "was full of plans for a new book. He was especially excited about a book he wanted to do on his experience in Ghana."[5] In their talks, Smith "mentioned . . . the famous encounter between James Baldwin and Richard Wright. He said he was the 'third party,' which Baldwin never mentions, whom Baldwin never identifies," and "Bill talked about a novel of which he had only the first 100 pages. He also mentioned his novel, "Simeon", which no publisher had yet taken."[6]

Bryant had, during their two meetings and correspondence, and through the article he had now published on Smith,[7] found a warm, receptive spot in Smith; he sent the only copy of "Simeon" to Bryant.[8] Bryant acknowledged receipt of the manuscript ten days later in a letter to Smith: "Yes, your copy of 'Simeon' did get here and it makes me nervous to have something like that in my responsibility. It's irreplaceable. I'll guard it carefully and get it back to [you] insured, the same way you got it to me. I haven't read it yet, but want to get to it before Christmas, and then back to you after the Christmas mail rush dies down. . . . Anyway, I'm grateful to you for sending it."[9] But the manuscript of "Simeon" was never received by Smith. Bryant says, "Everytime I think of the fact that the MS. is lost, I feel nauseous. . . . I can only speculate that in the first-of-the-year-mail from Denmark, the book disappeared."[10] Ironically, the previous year Smith had written Bryant, saying, "Since the writing of a book takes an average of one year, the five unfruitful years (representing the non-publication of books I knew were superior to the published ones) finally made me doubt myself. That, I presume, is the reason why, without meaning consciously to do so, I simply lost the manuscripts."[11]

Smith's reaction to the now lost-forever manuscript was simple: "He shrugged and refused to talk about it with anyone."[12]

Life continued in the Smiths' neighborhood of Ivry-sur-Seine, a suburb of Paris filled with blue-collar workers and foreign immigrants. By now, at the start of a new year, 1973, Rachel was nineteen months old, Claude was going on eight, and Michele would be ten in the coming October. Solange, who was recovering from a nervous breakdown some months earlier, was steadily improving.[13] Ira was getting ready to visit her father in India; her father was, perhaps, becoming blind, and wanted to see Ira and Rachel, at least once more.[14] Smith was still "at AFP, which is a grind," he said, "better than most but still a grind, but I have also begun work on a new book."[15] Also, "Doubleday Company [publishers] is apparently interested in the new book and I may soon sign a contract."[16] In a letter to his mother, he questioned: "Is Sonny [Doug, Jr.] participating in that barbarism unleashed against North Vietnam?" He went on, "I don't miss the States—I could never live there again, I think—but I do miss you and the warmth of the family." He closed the letter: "As for the country [America] itself, abroad it is gaining itself the reputation of another Nazi Germany through its actions in Vietnam. I am ashamed to show an American passport."

The year moved onward with Smith, now "the acknowledged dean of expatriate writers," working on the new book.[17] The working title of the nonfiction book was "Through Dark Eyes," begun in 1966.[18] He began outlining it again shortly after his second daughter's birth. "Through Dark Eyes" would tell the story of Smith's travels throughout three continents, North America, Europe, and Africa. About the proposed book, this much is known:

> What Bill really wanted to do was write a book called "Man Without A Country". This really reveals the real Bill, a man without a country.
>
> "Man Without A Country" was going to be a novel about a Black American who lives in France, who also lived in Africa, and because of these three continents—which all become part of him—he ceases to belong anywhere (which was really him), and he proposed this book to Doubleday who said that they were not interested in a novel. He was a journalist and knew many things which only a journalist would know at that time. So he switched the idea and worked it into "Through Dark Eyes." It was going to be nonfiction; it was going to be a long essay on the experiences of a Black man living in three continents and he wanted to bring into this the fact that through [his wife Ira] he had contact with another continent, with Asia, and to try to work this into it. He also had a sort of dream about Third World countries and Asia being part of the Third World countries—Asian solidarity with Africa.[19]

The year moved forward with Smith writing under financial pressure. "He was slowly getting 'uninvolved' with people, he ceased being sociable, with politics, with reading, with writing. He ceased to read books; people would send him books, which he'd then just put on the shelves. He'd lost his curiosity."[20] But his position at AFP kept him on the go.

Smith complained about internal pains to his friend, Dr. Jacques Tomasini. Tomasini recommended a complete medical examination, which was performed prior to a journalistic assignment in Algiers; the results would be completed while he was on assignment. On August 30, 1973, he departed for Algiers, remaining there for less than two weeks.[21] Upon his return was met by Dr. Tomasini, who informed him that, based on the test results, he had cancer. Smith immediately told Ira and, later, Solange of his condition. Surgery was scheduled for early December, but he had to return to Algiers on November 22 to complete his assignment. Back in Paris on November 30, Smith entered Hospital Lannelongue in early December.[22] He remained there almost three weeks; Tomasini informed Ira that it was a tiny tumor and that he was delighted with the results of the operation.[23]

In January and February 1974, Smith went to the French countryside to rest and recuperate. Later, he wrote to a friend:

> I have been out of work since December, and will return in mid-August or the beginning of September. The operation and treatment over the ensuing two weeks were hell, but the worst is over now. (They took out 20 centimetres of my esophagus; my stomach has been reduced to half its former size, and I have lost over 20 pounds.) Next week [early June] I begin six weeks of treatment by cobalt (five days of radiation per week, as an out-patient). Otherwise, I feel okay, though with far less strength and stamina than before. . . .
>
> It was odd, learning I had cancer. The doctor, a friend, who made the announcement to me when I returned from a reporting trip to Algeria, was far more shaken than I. It was a blow, but not really much of a surprise. . . . My doctor informed me that it was a very dangerous operation with an average 50 percent fatalities either on the operating table or in the 10 subsequent days (he told me this <u>after</u> the 10 days!), so I number among the lucky half. <u>I must</u> say that this doctor made sure that I had the best available specialists and treatment.[24]

But Smith waited until late July to write his family back in Philadelphia. The letter's content remains basically the same as the one written to his friend, adding that "I am ending up seven weeks of treatment by cobalt rays. In September, finally, I shall be permitted to return to work."[25]

During September, Smith's oldest sister, Phyllis, wrote to him. The letter, in part, concerned their mother's coming to Paris to see him. In response to the letter he wrote:

> I waited to get the results of the last medical tests before replying to you (it was good to hear from you; sorry I'm such a lousy letter writer). The answer is that Mom can wait until next summer before coming: I don't expect to be around for any old age pension, but I should certainly last through 1975! I prefer to have mother come during summer vacation rather than at Christmas: for one thing, I'll have more free time, and for another the weather is more agreeable. Winter in Paris can be pretty nasty.
>
> The cancer itself is no longer an immediate problem, but I am suffering from the effects of cobalt radio-therapy. I look like a skeleton, am always

> exhausted and out of breath, and in constant pain. I am going to the clinic today [October 3] for a one-week stay in which doctors will try to find how to ease this situation. But this is simply a matter of discomfort; there is no danger.
>
> Thanks for the photographs of your children.
>
> I look forward to Mom's forthcoming visit, and I hope to see the whole family anon.[26]

But Smith's expected short stay at the hospital, Clinique du Sud, at Thiais, not far from Paris, became much more than that. Upon reexamination it was decided that a second operation was required to find the cause of his constant pain. The diagnosis was that he was terminally ill of cancer. He was not informed of the results; his doctor, as well as his wife Ira, would never tell him. However, Smith seemed to know it. Ira would appear almost daily as he became weaker.[27]

On Tuesday, November 5, Ira went to the hospital at approximately 9:30 a.m. after taking her daughter to nursery school. She greeted her husband and sat down in the chair adjacent to the bed. Smith managed a slight smile, but the swelling of his face had almost completely closed off his vision. His face carried the signs of his pain, his discomfort. Ira spoke with him; he acknowledged her words. They were quiet for awhile and looked at television. Then Ira, realizing that she would have to get someone to baby-sit for their daughter, told him she would return if she could find someone. She left the clinic at approximately 3 p.m.[28]

Dr. Tomasini arrived a few minutes after Ira's departure to talk to Smith and check his condition. It was near 4 p.m., while Tomasini was talking to his friend and patient for less than two years, that Smith stopped breathing. Tomasini immediately applied all his medical knowledge in an effort to revive Smith, but the futile efforts were in vain. William Gardner Smith had died. Tomasini was in a state of shock. He had seen other patients die, but Smith was his friend.[29]

Meanwhile, Ira, upon leaving the hospital, had checked with several people to see if they would baby-sit. Her attempts to find someone proved fruitless, so she and Rachel finally went to the laundromat and completed some shopping. Dr. Tomasini wondered how to inform Ira of her husband's death. After almost three hours, he drove to the Smith's home, arriving at 7:30 p.m. He rang the doorbell, but Ira and Rachel were still out. He waited awhile, then departed.[30] Twelve hours later he rang the same doorbell. Opening the apartment door, Ira recognized Tomasini:

> I looked at him and he looked at me, and I knew. Standing at the door, he just nodded his head. Tomasini looked really haggard; I wouldn't be surprised if he hadn't been able to sleep.
>
> I said, "At what time? Was he alone?"
>
> "No," Tomasini said, "I was there."
>
> "Did he suffer?"

"No . . . It was as if he went to sleep."

"I'm glad," said Ira, as Tomasini finally entered the apartment.[31]

Paris was undergoing a telephone strike at the time of Smith's death. To contact his family immediately in Philadelphia was impossible. However, the day after his death, November 6, radio station KYW in Philadelphia, along with Westinghouse Broadcasting Company's eleven affiliate stations throughout the United States, reported his death.[32]

The news of his passing was heard by his cousin, Mrs. Barbara [Smith] Harris, on the radio. She immediately called Smith's mother's home. Sydney, his younger sister, answered the telephone. Shocked at hearing that her brother was dead, she called her sister Phyllis at her home. Phyllis called the radio station to verify the news broadcast and then rushed over to the South 20th Street address to comfort her sister and their mother when she returned home. Meanwhile, Barbara and her husband came to the home to be of additional comfort.[33]

Eventually, the always cheerful Mrs. Earle returned home to be greeted by a number of relatives. Not too sure of what was going on, she inquired. Phyllis broke the news of Smith's death to her. Stunned and amazed, but not really wanting to accept what she heard, Mrs. Edith Earle walked slowly toward the staircase leading upstairs to her bedroom without a sound.[34] The grief-stricken family looked to one another at the home Smith had lived in decades earlier. Details concerning the burial services would be worked out as more information was received from Ira in Paris.[35] The following day a telegram arrived from Ira confirming his death.[36]

Seven days after his death, services were held at Cimetière du Père Lachaise in Paris, where the offerings were conducted by Bernard Redmont. Several of Smith's personal friends, among the group of approximately seventy-five mourners, made public statements.[37] The services closed after Redmont read "Do Not Go Gentle into that Good Night," a poem by Dylan Thomas.[38] Smith was then cremated. His remains were placed in Crèche Number 15926 in the columbarian where, nearby, the remains of Richard Wright had been interred since early December 1960.[39]

On Saturday, November 23, 1974, at 2 p.m., services were conducted for William Gardner Smith at the Tasker Street Baptist Church in South Philadelphia. The mourners included the members of Smith's immediate family, Mary Sewell Smith, and a number of his lifelong friends. His brother and sister eulogized him. It was Phyllis who said, "The last time I saw him, characteristically, he was surrounded by people who had come to visit him while he was back here. Three of us went out to dinner with him and reminisced. Later, back home, in the house full of people again, I went upstairs to stay with him while he dressed. We talked quietly, like the old times."[40]

William Gardner Smith had now come full circle: birth, struggle for survival, accomplishment, death, and remembrance. Said one who knew him extremely well during his expatriate years: "He spent his life gritting his teeth, and we are all gritting our teeth for him now."[41]

Notes

CHAPTER 1

1. Miriam Ershkowitz and Joseph Zikmund II, eds., *Black Politics in Philadelphia* (New York: Basic Books, 1973), p. 13.
2. Ibid., p. 7.
3. Ibid., p. 13.
4. G. Gordon Brown, *Law Administration and Negro-White Relations in Philadelphia: A Study in Race Relations* (Philadelphia: Bureau of Municipal Research of Philadelphia, 1947), p. 52.
5. Ralph Ginzburg, *100 Years of Lynching* (New York: Lancer Books, 1962), p. 267.
6. Ershkowitz and Zikmund, *Black Politics in Philadelphia*, p. 24.
7. Ibid. pp. 55-56.
8. Ibid.
9. William Gardner Smith, *Return to Black America* (Englewood Cliffs, N. J.: Prentice-Hall, 1970), p. 5. "He [Douglas Stanley Earle, Sr.] was still a worker in a milk company where he had been employed for almost as long as I had known him." His title of "custodian" was given by Mrs. Edith Earle, his wife, during an interview on September 18, 1977.
10. Solange Royez, letter to author and response to questionnaire, July [18], 1977.
11. Ibid.
12. Wambly Bald, "Young Man Tackles Great Irony," *New York Post*, August 23, 1948.
13. FBI files, May 5, 1951, states that Smith's father is Leon Vernon Hemsley.
14. Joseph Bevans Bush, draft of "Memories of You(th), William Gardner Smith: A Writer of Importance," Philadelphia, undated [1977?].
15. Transcript of secondary school record [of Smith, William Gardner], Benjamin Franklin High School, Philadelphia.
16. Bush, "Memories of You(th)."

17. W. G. Smith, Letter to Carolyn Wolfe, April 8, 1949.
18. W. G. Smith, *Return to Black America*, p. 6.
19. Bald, "Young Man."
20. W. G. Smith, letter to Carolyn Wolfe, April 8, 1949.
21. William Gardner Smith, *The Stone Face* (New York: Farrar, Straus and Company, 1963), pp. 19-23.
22. Joseph Bevans Bush, "On Re-Calling William Gardner Smith: Writer and Friend," *Philadelphia Tribune*, August 30, 1977, p. 21.
23. W. G. Smith, *Return to Black America*, pp. 28-29.
24. Conversation with Mary Sewell Smith, May 28, 1977.
25. Nick Aaron Ford, "He Writes Novel at 20," *Afro Magazine Section*, October 30, 1948, p. 5.
26. Transcript of secondary school record.
27. Yearbook, Benjamin Franklin High School, Philadelphia, [1944?].
28. Transcript of secondary school record.
29. Ford, "He Writes Novel."
30. Jack Saunders, "Jack Saunders SAYS," *Philadelphia Tribune*, December 2, 1967, p. 8.
31. Ibid.
32. Bush, "Memories of You(th)."
33. W. G. Smith, letter to C. H. Williams, February 12, 1945.
34. Enlisted Record and Report of Separation-Honorable Discharge [Smith, William G.], February 19, 1947, item 31.
35. Bald, "Young Man," and "Navy Men Attack 'Courier' Reporter," *Pittsburgh Courier*, April 27, 1946, p. 5. Smith's companion was "later identified as Miss Valarie Rainey, daughter of Magistrate Joseph H. Rainey."
36. Bald, "Young Man."
37. Enlisted Record, item 6.
38. Army of the United States-Separation Qualification Record, February 19, 1947, item 13.
39. Bald, "Young Man."
40. Enlisted Record, item 7.
41. Ibid., item 47.
42. W. G. Smith, letter to Jerry Bryant, February 26, 1971. Also Bald "Young Man"; Ford, "He Writes Novel"; and "Author at Twenty," *Our World*, vol. 4, no. 1 (January 1949), pp. 40-42.
43. Transcript [William Gardner Smith], Office of Academic Records, Temple University, Philadelphia.
44. Appleton-Century Company, Inc., letter to William Gardner Smith, September 12, 1947.
45. John Farrar, Western Union telegram to William G. Smith, October 31, 1947.
46. Farrar, Straus and Company, letter to William G. Smith, October 31, 1947.
47. Ibid., December 4, 1947.
48. Ibid., December 16, 1947.
49. John Farrar and Roger Straus, Western Union telegram to William G. Smith, August 17, 1948.
50. William Gardner Smith, *Last of the Conquerors* (New York: Farrar, Straus and Company, 1948), 262 pp. Subsequent page references are indicated in parentheses after the quotations.
51. Ibid., p. 44. This passage is cited by Frank Rasky,

"Novels by Returned Veterans Are Sharp and Lean but Lack Scope," New York PM, August 15, 1948, and by Carl Milton Hughes, The Negro Novelist (New York: Citadel Press, 1953), p. 101.

52. W. G. Smith, Last of the Conquerors, p. 225. These two sentences appear to be the lines from which Smith derived the title "The Hammer and the Nail" for the manuscript of Last of the Conquerors.

53. Ilya Gregory, "Germany Meets the Negro Soldier," Ebony, vol. 1 no. 11 (October 1946), pp. 5-11. The author, Ilya Gregory, appears to be a psuedonym for William Gardner Smith. The names of the actual persons appearing in the article bear a striking resemblance to the novel's characters: "Capt. James Durkin of Chicago" seems to be "Captain Doyle of Chicago" in the novel; "T/5 Louis Dixon of Jersey City, New Jersey" is "Dixon from Jersey"; "Sgt. Austin Willis" as Austin Holmone (Homo)." Other striking similarities include the "truck outfit" in Berlin; and "German secretary Ann Muller" as "Ilse Mueller" is just too coincidental.

54. Jack Conroy, "Negro Soldier and Fraulein," Chicago Sun Times, August 17, 1948, p. 11.

55. Harrison Smith, "Land of Freedom?" Saturday Review of Literature, August 28, 1948, pp. 14-15.

56. Michael Bruen, "Negro Boy's Army Life in Germany," Dallas Times Herald, August 29, 1948, p. 11.

CHAPTER 2

1. Program, "Jerome Bowers Peterson Memorial Collection of Celebrated Negroes by Carl Van Vechten," Music and Art Salon, Wadleigh High School, New York, February 1949.

2. Program, "to bigotry—no sanction," Teachers Union of Philadelphia Local 556 U.P.W.-C.I.O., 4th Annual Conference and Luncheon, Philadelphia, March 5, 1949.

3. Nick Aaron Ford, "He Writes Novel at 20," Afro Magazine Section, October 30, 1948, p. 5.

4. John Praksta, "New Novelists Wanted to Be Actor," Temple University News, 1948; and "Author at Twenty," Our World, vol. 4, no. 1 (January 1949), p. 42.

5. Conversation with Mary Sewell Smith, November 23, 1978.

6. Ibid.

7. Anonymous.

8. Richard Gibson, letter to author, October 26, 1976.

9. Ibid.

10. Ibid.

11. Transcript [of William Gardner Smith], Office of Academic Records, Temple University, Philadelphia.

12. Mary Sewell Smith, November 23, 1978; Conrad Aiken, Selected Poems of Emily Dickinson (New York: Modern Library/Random House, 1924), p. 146.

13. John Farrar, letter to William G. Smith, September 7, 1948.

14. Ibid.

15. Roger W. Straus, Jr., letter to William G. Smith, February 17, 1949.

16. John Schaffner, letter to Carolyn Wolfe, September 14, 1949.

17. W. G. Smith, Western Union telegram to Arthur Orrmont, April 6, 1950.
18. W. G. Smith, letter to Arthur Orrmont, April 6, 1950.
19. Arthur Orrmont, letter to W. G. Smith, April 10, 1950.
20. Conversation with Arthur Orrmont, January 18, 1977.
21. Ibid.
22. William Gardner Smith, Anger at Innocence (New York: Farrar, Straus and Company, 1950), 300 pp. Subsequent page references are indicated in parentheses after the quotations.
23. Noel Schraufnagel, From Apology to Protest: The Black American Novel (Deland, Fla.: Everett/Edwards, 1973), p 63. Schraufnagel's definition of the "assimilationist novel" is as follows: "The assimilationist novels are in a sense a rejection of the limitations of the protest novel. By concentrating on whites, the writers are ostensibly free of the tendency to propagandize, and the white world with its multitudinous possibilities is open to them."
24. W. G. Smith, Anger at Innocence, p. 37. Rodina's "castle" and the building described as a "red brick tenement" seem to have been fused for Smith's unused title, "Red Brick Castle," for the manuscript of Anger at Innocence.
25. Carl Milton Hughes, The Negro Novelist (New York: Citadel Press, 1953), pp. 171-72.
26. Alain Locke, "Inventory at Mid-Century: A Review of the Literature of the Negro for 1950," Phylon, vol. XII, no. 1 (First Quarter 1951), pp. 7-8.
27. Robert Kingery, Library Journal, Ocotober 1, 1950, p. 1662.

CHAPTER 3

1. Richard Gibson, letter to author, April 13, 1977.
2. Anonymous.
3. William Gardner Smith, letter to Edith Earle, March 14, 1952.
4. FBI files, May 5, 1951; and US State Department files, December 4, 1951.
5. US State Department files, September 21, 1951.
6. Conversation with Mary Sewell Smith, August 27, 1977.
7. W. G. Smith, letter Edith Earle, October 16, 1951.
8. Ibid.
9. Layna Verin, letter to author, January 3, 1978.
10. Ibid.
11. Roi Ottley, "Black Frenchmen," Negro Digest, February 1948, p. 20.
12. Ibid.
13. Ibid., p. 22.
14. Richard Wright, "American Negroes in France," Crisis, no. 58 (June-July 1951), p. 381; first published as "Les Noirs Américans et la France" in France-Observateur, no. 56 (May 3, 1951).
15. Michel Fabre, The Unfinished Quest of Richard Wright. (New York: William Morrow & Co., 1973), pp. 300, 308.
16. Ibid., p. 310.
17. Ibid., p. 312.

18. Ibid., pp. 312-13.
19. Wright, "American Negroes," pp. 382-83.
20. Conversation with Harry Goldberg, June 15, 1978; and conversation with Mary Sewell Smith, May 28, 1977.
21. W. G. Smith, letter to Edith Earle, November 1, 1951.
22. Ibid.
23. Ibid.
24. Ibid.
25. Ibid.
26. Ibid., December 20, 1951.
27. Ibid.
28. US State Department files, December 8, 1951.
29. W. G. Smith, "European Backdrop," Pittsburgh Courier, January 5, 1952, p. 3.
30. W. G. Smith, letter to Edith Earle, March 12, 1952.
31. W. G. Smith, Pittsburgh Courier, May 31, 1952, p. 4.
32. Anonymous.
33. W. G. Smith, "The Oldest Negro in Paris," Ebony, vol. VII, no. 12 (October 1952), pp. 65-66, 68-72. Article deals with the life of Charles Anderson, American-born Negro, aged 91, who left America in 1884 and never returned. Anderson was born on March 15, 1861 in Lebanon, Illinois.
34. W. G. Smith, "Black Boy in France," Ebony, vol. VIII, no. 9 (July 1953) pp. 32-36, 39-42. Article deals with life of Richard Wright in Paris over a span of seven years.
35. Ibid., p. 41; and see Edward Margolies, The Art of Richard Wright (Carbondale and Edwardsville, Ill.: Southern Illinois University Press, 1969), p. 123.
36. "Amid the Alien Corn," Time, November 17, 1958, p. 28.
37. W. G. Smith, letter to Edith Earle, February 21, 1953.
38. Conversation with Harry Goldberg, June 15, 1978.
39. W. G. Smith, letter to Edith Earle, February 21, 1953.
40. Chester Himes, The Quality of Hurt (New York: Doubleday, 1972), p. 185.
41. Ibid., pp. 247-48.
42. W. G. Smith, letter to Edith Earle, February 21, 1953.
43. Himes, Quality of Hurt, pp. 189-90.
44. US State Department files, September 28, 1953.
45. W. G. Smith, letter to Edith Earle, February 21, 1953.
46. William Gardner Smith, South Street (New York: Farrar, Straus and Young, 1954), 312 pp. Subsequent page references are indicated in parentheses after the quotations.
47. W. G. Smith, letter to John Farrar, undated [February 1954?].
48. W. G. Smith, letter to Jerry Bryant, February 26, 1971.
49. South Street, p. 17. This reference to Richard Wright may have inadvertently annoyed Wright and placed further strain on the fragile "friendship" of Smith and Wright. Chester Himes, The Quality of Hurt (New York: Doubleday, 1972), p. 185, writes that as early as April 1953 "it was very obvious [Smith] and Dick [Wright] did not like each other at all."
50. Noel Schraufnagel, From Apology to Protest: The Black American Novel (Deland, Fla.: Everett Edwards, 1973), pp. 114-15, 173-74, 200.

51. This is my speculation based on the verbal outline of "Simeon" as explained during an interview with Ira Gardner Smith, July 16, 1978.
52. Henry F. Winslow, "High Fidelity," _Crisis_, February 1955, pp. 124-25.
53. Gilbert Millstein, "The Problem as Before," _New York Times Book Review_, October 81, 1954, p. 34.
54. Doris Dungill Holmes, "Story of Any Negro," _Phylon_, vol. XVI, no. 1 (First Quarter 1955), pp. 115-17.

CHAPTER 4

1. William Gardner Smith, letter to Edith Earle, June 17, 1955.
2. Joseph Barry, "An American in Paris—II," _New York Post_, March 25, 1959, p. 36.
3. Ibid.
4. Conversation with Musy Hafner, July 24, 1978.
5. Frank Van Brakle, letter to _Jet_ magazine, June 4, 1958.
6. William Gardner Smith, _Return to Black America_, (Englewood Cliffs, N. J.: Prentice-Hall, 1970), pp. 59-60; and David Bakish, _Richard Wright_, (New York: Frederick Unger Publishing Co., 1973), p. 56.
7. Conversation with Musy Hafner, July 24, 1978.
8. Harry Goldberg, letter to author, October 12, 1976.
9. Solange Royez, letter to author and response to questionnaire, July [18,] 1977. To the question: "Bill's position concerning the Algerian War?" her answer was: "Bill felt in complete solidarity with the Algerian FLN [and] it is clear in _[The] Stone Face_."
10. W. G. Smith, letter to Edith Earle, June 17, 1955.
11. "Simeon" was first mentioned in Smith's letter to John Farrar, undated [February 1954?]. Subsequent correspondence during this period suggests this date, February 1954: "a delay in publication of SIMEON, which is finished," is cited in a letter to Farrar from Naomi Burton of Curtis Brown, Ltd., on March 29, 1954.
12. Conversation with Ira Gardner Smith, July 16, 1978.
13. Anonymous.
14. W. G. Smith, letter to John Farrar, undated [February 1954?].
15. Ibid., [May 1954?]. Smith wrote: "I wish I had received your notes on _South Street_ before writing SIMEON; the former would have helped me very much with the latter. . . . I tried on purpose to slow down the movement of SIMEON and put more flesh on the plot bones."
16. New American Library of World Literature, letter to Roger W. Straus, Jr., May 13, 1954.
17. John Farrar, Letter to Naomi Burton, May 24, 1954.
18. Ibid.
19. W. G. Smith, letter to John Farrar, undated [June 1954?].
20. I. G. Smith, July 16, 1978. There is the possibility that the manuscript was with papers Smith had stored in suitcases in the basement of his Ivry-sur-Seine residence. However,

subsequent to Smith's death, his personal effects were stolen from his basement bin or storage space. Alternatively, the manuscript may have been lost; Smith mentions that "all manuscripts [were] lost in travel" in a letter to Jerry Bryant on February 26, 1971. It is interesting to note that the "outline that [Smith] sent of THE GANGSTERS is good but it would be only good if he managed to give it the plus quality of both feeling and writing that is minus in SIMEON" (John Farrar, letter to Naomi Burton, May 24, 1954).

21. W. G. Smith, letter to Edith Earle, June 17, 1955.
22. Richard Gibson, letter to author, October 26, 1976.
23. Ibid.
24. Ibid.
25. Ibid., July 7, 1977.
26. Ibid., October 26, 1976.
27. Ibid.
28. This remains a total mystery. The person closest to Smith during 1955 was Musy Hafner. Interviewed on July 24, 1978, she states she did not know when Smith's passport was taken or when it was returned. Smith, in a letter to his mother on September 18, 1964—he was now in Ghana—alluded to the passport mystery by writing, "You must know that your oldest son's political ideas are not much liked by the State Department; they took my passport away from me once, and they might do it again if I returned [to the US]. I must not take any chances." Michel Fabre, in his biography of Richard Wright, The Unfinished Quest of Richard Wright (New York: William Morrow & Co., 1973), p. 463, writes of the treatment afforded expatriates in "the 'witch hunt' mood in Paris during the mid-fifties . . . reinforced by . . . the head of the passport bureau at the American Embassy, [who] could decide the fate of anyone too progressive or incautious." Richard Gibson states, "The [American] Embassy did not approve of black people hanging around France [during the 1950's]," in a letter to author, June 27, 1977. Moreover, State Department files indicate that on September 28, 1953, Smith's passport was "renewed for two years to expire on September 26, 1955." For a period of almost two years Smith did not possess a valid passport.
29. Musy Hafner, July 24, 1978.
30. Conversation with Mary Sewell Smith, November 25, 1978.
31. Fabre, Unfinished Quest, p. 461.
32. US State Department files, May 2, 1957.
33. Ibid.
34. Ibid., May 15, 1957, June 7, 1957, and July 9, 1962.
35. Fabre, Unfinished Quest. While Fabre states that Harrington "was away on the Côte d'Azur," Gibson states that "Harrington went to Sweden, not the Côte d'Azur" in a letter to author, June 26, 1977.
36. Fabre, Unfinished Quest.
37. Gibson, June 26, 1977.
38. Fabre, Unfinished Quest, p. 462.
39. Ibid.
40. Royez, July [18,] 1977.
41. Fabre, Unfinished Quest: ". . . since his arrival in

1955" is apparently a typographical error; Harrington is cast as being in Paris "by 1953" on p. 382. Additionally, Chester Himes, in his autobiography, The Quality of Hurt (New York: Doubleday, 1972), p. 178, states that Harrington was to have met Himes upon his arrival in Paris on April 11, 1953. Smith, however, lists Harrington even earlier in "European Backdrop," Pittsburgh Courier, May 24, 1952, p. 20, where he writes: "Ollie Harrington in town, just down the street, in a good old Latin Quarter." Further, Harrington's "Dark Laughter" cartoon appears in the Courier of July 19, 1952 with "Paris" listed after his name.

42. "Master of the Sex Story," Modern Man, vol. VI, no. 4-64 (October 1956), pp. 10-11, 55-56.

43. "Europe's Naked Nature Boy," Modern Man, vol. VI, no. 6-66 (December 1956), pp. 38-41, 56.

44. Fabre, Unfinished Quest, p. 479.

45. Editorials, "Hopeful Plan for Algeria," Life, September 30, 1957, p. 32.

46. Letters to the editor, Editorials, Life, October 21, 1957, p. 10.

47. Fabre, Unfinished Quest, p. 462.

48. Ibid.

49. Gibson, October 26, 1976.

50. Fabre, Unfinished Quest.

51. Gibson, June 26, 1977.

52. Ibid.

53. Ibid.

54. Ibid.

55. Fabre, Unfinished Quest.

56. Ibid., p. 463.

57. Ibid.

58. My source for Richard Wright's notes and papers are in the possession of Michel Fabre. Mary Sewell Smith denies ever sleeping with Gibson in an interview with author on May 28, 1977. Gibson also denies having an affair with Mary and writes: "Sometimes, jokingly, I thought, [Smith] referred to me to people in Paris years afterward, as my wife's lover" (letter to author, October 26, 1976). In another letter Gibson states: "Mary and I got together . . . in the States, while I was in the U.S. Army [at Fort Dix, N.J.] in 1953, and I got to Philadelphia often on weekends and saw a lot of Mary" (June 24, 1977).

59. Van Brakle, June 4, 1978.

60. Gibson, October 26, 1976. Italics added.

61. Ibid. It should be noted, however, that my assessment is based on circumstantial evidence. I have only Gibson's word that his federal employment, in any capacity, was his military service. During a number of interviews in Paris, for instance, most respondents did not trust Gibson or anything he says.

62. Addison Gayle, Richard Wright: Ordeal of a Native Son (Garden City, N.Y.: Anchor Press/Doubleday, 1980), p. 283.

63. William G. Smith, "The World's Most Famous Nude," Art and Photography, vol. VIII, no. 10-94 (April 1957), pp. 14-15, 43-45. Musy Hafner states that she did most of the research for

three of Smith's articles: "Master of the Sex Story," "Europe's Naked Nature Boy," and "The World's Most Famous Nude" (interview with author, July 24 1978).

64. "The Fraulein and the Private," *Duke*, July 1957, pp. 9-11, 65-66. This is a carefully edited article extracting, in part, sensuous portions of *Last of the Conquerors*, pp. 44-50, 53-56, 85-91.

65. "Amid the Alien Corn," *Time*, November 17, 1958, p. 28.

66. Ibid.

67. Gibson, October 26, 1976.

68. "Amid the Alien Corn."

69. Barry, "American in Paris."

70. Musy Hafner, July 24, 1978.

71. Royez, July [18,] 1977.

72. W. G. Smith, letter to Mary Sewell Smith, October 17, 1959.

73. Foreign money order receipt, no. 8252257, American Express Company, October 29, 1959.

74. Conversation with Solange Royez, June 11, 1978.

75. Conversation with Mary Sewell Smith, November 23, 1978.

76. W. G. Smith, letter to Mary Sewell Smith, July 5, 1960.

77. Ibid.

78. Ibid.

79. "Amid the Alien Corn."

80. Fabre, *Unfinished Quest*, pp. 517-19.

81. Musy Hafner, July 24, 1978. "We both shuddered at the sound of Wright's burning body, quite audible in the still Columbarium," she said.

82. W. G. Smith, "The Compensation for the Wound," *Two Cities*, no. 6 (Summer 1961), pp. 67-69.

83. Royez, letter to author, July [18,] 1977; and W. G. Smith, letter to Mary Sewell Smith, October 17, 1959.

84. Anonymous. The new novel, untitled, was to center on an integrated couple.

85. W. G. Smith, letter to Edith Earle, July 25, 1961.

86. Ibid.

87. Royez, July [18,] 1977.

88. W. G. Smith, letter to Edith Earle, undated [1962?].

89. Solange [Royez] Smith, letter to Edith Earle, July 18, 1962.

90. Ibid.

91. Solange Royez, June 11, 1978.

92. W. G. Smith, letter to Edith Earle, undated [1962?].

93. Ibid., April 20, 1963.

94. William Gardner Smith, *The Stone Face* (New York: Farrar, Straus and Company, 1963), 213 pp. Subsequent page references are indicated in parentheses after the quotations.

95. Clearly, the character of Simeon Brown is Smith. The fictionalized Howard seems to be classical composer Howard Swanson, while Chester Himes is apparently "James Benson." "Babe Carter" is a combination of Richard Wright-Ollie Harrington-Leroy Haynes, mostly Wright. "Doug" appears to be Richard Gibson. (All identities are my speculation.)

96. W. G. Smith, *Stone Face*, p. 87. Smith poses an interesting question.

97. John Farrar, letter to William G. Smith, January 9, 1963.
98. W. G. Smith, letter to Roger W. Straus, July 11, 1963.
99. J. Farrar, letter to William G. Smith, July 24, 1963, and W. G. Smith, letter to Roger W. Straus, August 6, 1963.
100. Joseph Friedman, "The Unvarying Visage of Hatred," *New York Times Book Review*, November 17, 1963, p. 53.
101. Jean Carey Bond, "Excellent Ideas in Search of Greater Skill," *Freedomways*, vol. IV, no. 2 (Spring 1964), pp. 272-74.
102. Nick Aaron Ford, "The Fire Next Time? A Critical Survey of Belles Lettres By and About Negroes Published in 1963," *Phylon*, vol. XXV, no. 2 (Summer 1964), pp. 123-26.

CHAPTER 5

1. William Gardner Smith, letter to Phyllis Earle, February 17, 1964.
2. Solange Royez, letter to author, July [18,] 1977.
3. Ibid.
4. Shirley Graham Du Bois, "What Happened In Ghana? The Inside Story," *Freedomways*, no. 3 (Summer 1966), pp. 203-5.
5. Kwame Nkrumah, *Dark Days in Ghana* (New York: International Publishers, 1968), p. 41.
6. Ibid.
7. W. G. Smith, letter to Edith Earle, January 9, 1964.
8. W. G. Smith, letter to Phyllis Earle, February 17, 1964.
9. Solange Smith, letter to Edith Earle, April 3, 1964.
10. Ibid., April 6, 1964.
11. "Then and Now," *Paris Review*, vol. IX, no. 33 (Winter-Spring 1965), p. 158. Also see "The 'Lost' Generation Meets Its Epigoni," *Paris Gazette*, May 24-May 30, 1964.
12. "Then and Now."
13. Ibid., pp. 164-66.
14. W. G. Smith, letter to Edith Earle, September 18, 1964.
15. Peter Goldman, *The Death and Life of Malcolm X* (New York: Perennial Library, 1974), p. 196.
16. Ibid.
17. Ibid.
18. Ann Allen Shockley and Sue P. Chandler, *Living Black American Authors* (New York: R. R. Bowker Co., 1973), pp. 4, 49-50, 89, 92, 107-8.
19. William Gardner Smith, *Return to Black America* (Englewood Cliffs, N.J.: Prentice-Hall, 1970), pp. 95-96.
20. Goldman, *Malcolm X*, p. 239.
21. Ibid.
22. Ibid., 239-40.
23. Ibid., p. 240.
24. Ibid.
25. Ibid.
26. Royez, July [18,] 1977.
27. W. G. Smith, *Return to Black America*, pp. 96-98.
28. Julian Mayfield, letter to author, January 10, 1977.
29. Ibid.
30. Ibid.
31. Conversation with Solange Royez, June 11, 1978.

32. Ibid.
33. Goldman, Malcolm X, pp. 298-99.
34. Ibid., p. 278.
35. W. G. Smith, letter to Edith Earle, June 7, 1965.
36. Ibid.
37. St. Clair Drake, "Nkrumah: The Real Tragedy," Nation, vol. CCXIV, no. 23 (June 5, 1972), p. 723.
38. Ibid., p. 724.
39. W. G. Smith, Return to Black America, p. 99.
40. Ibid.
41. W. G. Smith, letter to Phyllis Earle, November 10, 1965.
42. Nkrumah, Dark Days, p. 13; and Du Bois, "What Happened," p. 213.
43. Du Bois, "What Happened," p. 213.
44. Nkrumah, Dark Days, p. 49.
45. Ibid.
46. Du Bois, "What Happened," p. 213.
47. Conversation with Solange Royez, June 11, 1978.
48. Ibid.
49. Ibid.

CHAPTER 6

1. William Gardner Smith, letter to Edith Earle, March 23, 1966.
2. W. G. Smith, letter to Phyllis Earle, April 4, 1966. And see note 6, below.
3. Solange Smith, letter to Edith Earle, October 20, 1966.
4. Ibid.
5. Ibid.
6. Smith's estimation of American CIA involvement in Nkrumah's downfall was correct. See John Stockwell, In Search of Enemies (New York: W. W. Norton & Company, 1978), p. 201; and Seymour H. Hersh, "C.I.A. Said to Have Aided Plotters Who Overthrew Nkrumah in Ghana," New York Times, May 9, 1978, p. 6.
7. W. G. Smith, letter to Roger W. Straus, January 31, 1967.
8. W. G. Smith, Western Union telegram to Edith Earle, July 29, 1967.
9. W. G. Smith, letter to Edith Earle, September 9, 1967. (Smith spoke to Douglas, Jr., by phone)
10. Telephone conversation with Mary Sewell Smith, January 12, 1979.
11. Telephone conversation with Phyllis [Earle] Ford, January 18, 1979.
12. Conversation with Mary Sewell Smith, November 25, 1978; and W. G. Smith, letter to Edith Earle, September 9, 1967.
13. W. G. Smith, letter to Edith Earle, September 9, 1967.
14. Joe Hunter, Guest Columnist, "Jack Saunders SAYS," Philadelphia Tribune, September 23, 1967, p. 8.
15. W. G. Smith, letter to Mary Sewell Smith, September 28, 1967.
16. Ibid.
17. Ibid.; also letters to Roger W. Straus on January 9, 1967, and June 1, 1967.

18. Herbert R. Lottman, letter to Roger W. Straus, December 1, 1967.
19. W. G. Smith, letter to Mary Sewell Smith, April 15, 1968.
20. Ibid.; and William Gardner Smith, Return to Black America (Englewood Cliffs, N.J.: Prentice-Hall, 1970), p. 5.
21. W. G. Smith, letter to Mary Sewell Smith, April 15, 1968.
22. Herbert R. Lottman, "The Last Indian Jews," Present Tense, vol. III, no. 4 (Summer 1976), p. 7.
23. Conversation with Ira Gardner Smith, July 16, 1978.
24. Lottman, "Indian Jews," p. 9.
25. Solange Royez, letter to author, July [18,] 1977.
26. W. G. Smith, Return to Black America, 185 pp. Subsequent page references are indicated in parentheses after the quotations.
27. O. A. Bouise, Best Sellers, July 1, 1970, p. 140.
28. New Yorker, April 25, 1970, p. 137.
29. W. G. Smith, letter to Edith Earle, December 30, 1972.
30. William Gardner Smith, L'Amérique Noire (Tournai, Belgium: Casterman, S.A., 1972), 150 pp.

CHAPTER 7

1. William Gardner Smith, letter to Jerry Bryant, February 26, 1971.
2. FBI files, November 9, 1971: "arrived Miami . . . via Braniff . . . Airlines, Flight 974 . . . originated Buenos Aires."
3. W. G. Smith, letter to Edith Earle, July 22, 1972.
4. Jerry Bryant, letter to author, August 5, 1976.
5. Ibid.
6. Ibid.
7. Jerry H. Bryant, "Individuality and Fraternity: The Novels of William Gardner Smith," Studies in Black Literature, vol. III, no. 2 (Summer 1972), pp. 1-8.
8. W. G. Smith, letter to Jerry Bryant, December 4, 1972.
9. Bryant, letter to William Gardner Smith, December 14, 1972.
10. Bryant, letter to author, August 5, 1976.
11. W. G. Smith, letter to Jerry Bryant, February 26, 1971.
12. Conversation with Ira Gardner Smith, July 16, 1978.
13. W. G. Smith, letter to Edith Earle, December 30, 1972.
14. Ibid.
15. Ibid.
16. Ibid.
17. Herbert R. Lottman, "The Action Is Everywhere the Black Man Goes," New York Times Book Review, April 21, 1968, p. 7; Stanley Schatt, "You Must Go Home Again: Today's Afro-American Expatriate Writers," Negro American Literature Forum, vol. VII, no. 3 (Fall 1973), p. 80; and Ishbel Ross, The Expatriates (New York: Thomas Y. Crowell Company, 1970), p. 292.
18. W. G. Smith, letter to Roger W. Straus, January 9, 1967. In the letter Smith states: "I could have sent this outline ["Through Dark Eyes"] off months ago; but I had been trying to send along also 50 to 100 pages of the book." [A six-page outline is attached to the letter.] On June 1, 1967, he

forwarded "the first two chapters of the book, which will give you an idea of the style and tone," to Straus, a total of twenty pages.

19. Ira Gardner Smith, July 16, 1978.
20. Ibid.
21. US passport no. Z1832459, issued to William Gardner Smith on August 8, 1973, p. 7.
22. Ira Gardner Smith, July 16, 1978.
23. Ibid.
24. W. G. Smith, letter to Celia Hornung Sanders, May 30, 1974.
25. W. G. Smith, letter to Edith Earle, July 24, 1974.
26. W. G. Smith, letter to Phyllis [Earle] Ford, October 3, 1974.
27. Ira Gardner Smith, July 16, 1978.
28. Ibid.
29. Ibid.
30. Ibid.
31. Ibid.
32. Bernard Redmont, letter to Edith Earle, November 19, 1974. Attached to letter was a transcript of his radio message and a copy of the testimonial to Smith given at Pere Lachaise Cemetery.
33. Conversation with Sydney Earle, November 25, 1978.
34. Ibid.
35. Ibid.
36. Ibid.
37. Redmont, "Memorial for William Gardner Smith," November 12, 1974.
38. Ibid., poem from Dylan Thomas, *In Country Sleep* (New York: New Directions Books, 1952), pp. 18-19.
39. Constance Webb, *Richard Wright: A Biography* (New York: G. P. Putnam's Sons, 1968), p. 400.
40. Phyllis [Earle] Ford, copy of eulogy given on November 23, 1974, at Tasker Street Baptist Church, Philadelphia.
41. Solange Royez, letter to author, July [18,] 1977.

Bibliography

WILLIAM GARDNER SMITH'S PUBLISHED WORKS

Fiction

Last of the Conquerors, New York: Farrar, Straus and Company, 1948. 262 pp.
Anger at Innocence, New York: Farrar, Straus and Company, 1950. 300 pp.
South Street, New York: Farrar, Straus and Young, 1954. 312 pp.
The Stone Face, New York: Farrar, Straus and Company, 1963. 213 pp.

Nonfiction

Books

Return to Black America, Englewood Cliffs, N.J.: Prentice-Hall, 1970. 185 pp.

Articles and essays

"A Phylon Profile, XXI: Ethel Waters." *Phylon*, vol. XI, no. 2 (Second Quarter 1950), pp. 114-20.
"The Negro Writer: Pitfalls and Compensations." *Phylon*, vol. XI, no. 4 (Fourth Quarter 1950), pp. 297-303.
"The Oldest Negro in Paris." *Ebony*, vol. VIII, no. 12 (October 1952), pp. 65-66, 68-72.
"Black Boy in France." *Ebony*, vol. VIII, no. 9 (July 1953), pp. 32-36, 38-42.
"Master of the Sex Story." *Modern Man*, vol. VI, no. 4-64 (October 1956), pp. 10-11, 55-56.
"Europe's Naked Nature Boy." *Modern Man*, vol. VI, no. 6-66 (December 1956), pp. 38-41, 56.
"The World's Most Famous Nude." *Art and Photography*, vol. VIII,

no. 10-94 (April 1957), pp. 14-15, 43-45.
"The Compensation for the Wound." Two Cities, no. 6 (Summer 1961), pp. 67-69.
"Black Man in Europe." Holiday, vol. 37, no. 1 (January 1965), pp. 22. 24-26, 28-29.
"The Gangs Have Changed." Pittsburgh Inquirer Magazine, July 26, 1970, pp. 12-15. (Extracted from Return to Black America, pp. 28-36.)

Newspaper Reporting and Journalism

"Negroes in Germany Set Styles Until Nazis Started Hatred Drive." Pittsburgh Courier, September 7, 1946, p. 13.
"General McNarney Ignores Gillem Report, Isolates GIs." Pittsburgh Courier, October 26, 1946, pp. 1, 4.
"Army 'Big Shots' Speed 'Purge' of Race Troops from Germany." Pittsburgh Courier, November 9, 1946, p. 3.
"Half of Tan GIs Leaving Germany." Pittsburgh Courier, December 21, 1946, pp. 1, 4.
"Found Freedom in Germany: Few GIs Eager to Return to States." Pittsburgh Courier, February 22, 1947, pp. 1, 4.
"Keeping the Peace: American Prejudice Rampant in Germany." Pittsburgh Courier, March 1, 1947, p. 13.
"New Trials for 6 Men." Pittsburgh Courier, July 9, 1949, pp. 1, 5.
"European Backdrop (The life of Paris is in cafes)." Pittsburgh Courier, January 5, 1952, p. 3.
"European Backdrop (The people you meet in Paris)." Pittsburgh Courier, January 12, 1952, p. 2.
"European Backdrop (Katherine Dunham). "Pittsburgh Courier, January 19, 1952, p. 3.
"European Backdrop (Hazel Scott)." Pittsburgh Courier, January 26, 1952, p. 3.
"Average European Visualized U.S. as Being a 'Land of Terror.'" Pittsburgh Courier, January 26, 1952, p. 13.
"European Backdrop (You don't change personalities)." Pittsburgh Courier, February 2, p. 9.
"American Negroes in Europe Mingle with 'In-Betweens.'" Pittsburgh Courier, February 2, p. 13.
"European Colonials Feel Superior to U.S. Negroes." Pittsburgh Courier, February 9, 1952, p. 13.
"U.S. Caste System Makes Race Inferior to Poorest of European." Pittsburgh Courier, February 16, 1952, p. 13.
"European Backdrop (When you feel in the Harlem mood)." Pittsburgh Courier, February 16, 1952, p. 13.
"European Backdrop (If you've got a certain brand of humor)." Pittsburgh Courier, February 23, 1952, p. 12.
"European Backdrop (Edith Sampson's views fail to click with students)." Pittsburgh Courier, March 8, 1952, p. 2.
"European Backdrop (M. Alione Diop)." Pittsburgh Courier, March 15, 1952, p. 12.
"European Backdrop (London is the largest city)." Pittsburgh Courier, April 5, 1952, p. 13.
"European Backdrop (Report from Rome)." Pittsburgh Courier,

April 12, 1952, p. 13.
"European Backdrop (As this appears . . . from Paris)." Pittsburgh Courier, April 19, 1952, p. 12.
"European Backdrop (It was a touching gesture)." Pittsburgh Courier, April 26, 1952, p. 12
"European Backdrop (Renee Maran)." Pittsburgh Courier, May 3, 1952, p. 12.
"European Backdrop (One brief insight)." Pittsburgh Courier, May 10, 1952, p. 12.
"European Backdrop (London--We, who are Negroes)." Pittsburgh Courier, May 17, 1952, p. 12.
"La Scala Opera Co. Will Hire Spelman Soprano This Fall." Pittsburgh Courier, May 24, 1952, p. 3.
"European Backdrop (Dizzy Gillespie)." Pittsburgh Courier, May 24, 1952, p. 20.
"Friend Reveals Hate Hurt Canada [Lee] Deeply." Pittsburgh Courier, May 31, 1952, pp. 1, 4.
"European Backdrop (Report from Germany)." Pittsburgh Courier, May 31, 1952, p. 13.
"Africans Figure in Paris Riots." Pittsburgh Courier, June 7, 1952, p. 5.
"European Backdrop (Report from Africa-I)." Pittsburgh Courier, June 7, 1952, p. 12.
"European Backdrop (Report from Africa-II)." Pittsburgh Courier, June 14, 1952, p. 20.
"European Backdrop (There are three souls)." Pittsburgh Courier, June 21, 1952, p. 12.
"European Backdrop (The party was fabulous)." Pittsburgh Courier, June 28, 1952, p. 22.
"European Backdrop (The pleasures of Paris)." Pittsburgh Courier, July 5, 1952, p. 12.
"European Backdrop (Ligon Buford)." Pittsburgh Courier, July 12, 1952, p. 12.
"European Backdrop (Music on the town)." Pittsburgh Courier, July 19, 1952, p. 20.
"European Backdrop (More American Negro women)." Pittsburgh Courier, July 26, 1952, p. 20.
"Many Ex-GIs Wandering Illegally Through Europe." Pittsburgh Courier, August 2, 1952, p. 3.
"European Backdrop (There's a lot of loose . . .)." Pittsburgh Courier, August 2, 1952, p. 3.
"European Backdrop (Man in search of a story)." Pittsburgh Courier, August 9, 1952, p. 12.
"European Backdrop (The students lead)." Pittsburgh Courier, August 16, 1952, p. 12.
"European Backdrop (The "Purda")." Pittsburgh Courier, August 23, 1952, p. 20.
"European Backdrop (August in Paris)." Pittsburgh Courier, August 30, 1952, p. 12.
"European Backdrop (The Felix Eboüse Story)." September 13, 1952, p. 12.
"European Backdrop (The death of an institution)." Pittsburgh Courier, September 20, 1952. p. 12.
"European Backdrop (The Rome scene)." Pittsburgh Courier,

September 27, 1952, p. 12.
"European Backdrop (The headlines speak)." Pittsburgh Courier, October 4, 1952, p. 20.

BOOKS CITING DATA ON THE LIFE AND CAREER OF WILLIAM GARDNER SMITH

Bakish, David. Richard Wright. New York: Frederick Unger Publishing Co., 1973, p. 56.

Bigsby, C. W. E., ed. The American Writer. Volume I: Fiction. Deland, Fla.: Everett/Edwards, 1969, pp. 241-42.

Bone, Robert. The Negro Novel in America. New Haven: Yale University Press, 1958.

Dunbar, Ernest. The Black Expatriates. New York: E. P. Dutton & Co., 1968, p. 7.

Fabre, Michel. The Unfinished Quest of Richard Wright. New York: William Morrow & Co., 1973, pp. 462-63, 471-72, 475, 479.

Gayle, Addison, Jr., ed. Black Expression. New York: Weybright and Talley, 1969. Contains three articles citing Smith: Nick Aaron Ford, "A Blueprint for Negro Authors," pp. 276-80; Gayle, "Perhaps Not So Soon One Morning," pp. 280-88; and Smith, "The Negro Writer: Pitfalls and Compensations," pp. 288-95.

———. The Way of the New World: The Black Novel in America. Garden City, N.Y.: Anchor Books/Doubleday, 1976, pp. xx, 123, 192, 201, 232, 239-47, 381.

———. Richard Wright: Ordeal of a Native Son. Garden City, N.Y.: Anchor Press/Doubleday, 1980, pp. 199, 225-26, 229, 231, 234. Gayle claims Smith had "begun his exile around 1948"; Smith actually arrived in France on October 19, 1951.

Hemenway, Robert. The Black Novelist. Columbus, Ohio: Charles E. Merrill Publishing Company, 1970. Contains mention of Smith in Introduction; also Smith, "The Negro Writer--Pitfalls and Compensations," pp. 196-204.

Himes, Chester. The Quality of Hurt. Volume I. Garden City, N.Y.: Doubleday, 1972, pp. 185, 189-90, 247-49.

———. My Life of Absurdity. Volume II. Garden City, N.Y.: Doubleday, 1976, pp. 2, 73, 123, 144, 158, 163-64, 185, 193-94, 217, 221.

Lacy, Leslie Alexander. The Rise and Fall of a Proper Negro. New York: Macmillan Co., 1970, p. 234.

Lottman, Herbert R. The Left Bank. Boston: Houghton Mifflin Company, 1982, pp. 245-46.

Lundquist, James. Chester Himes. New York: Frederick Unger Publishing Co., 1976, pp. 21-22, 73.

Margolies, Edward. The Art of Richard Wright. Carbondale and Edwardsville, Ill.: Southern Illinois University Press, 1969, p. 123.

McCall, Dan. The Example of Richard Wright. New York: Harcourt, Brace & World, 1969, p. 138.

Nicholas, Charles H., ed. Arna Bontemps-Langston Hughes Letters. New York: Dodd, Mead & Company, 1980, pp. 255, 257, 281.

Shockley, Ann Allen and Sue P. Chandler. Living Black American Authors. New York: R. R. Bowker Co., 1973, p. 148.

Webb, Constance. Richard Wright: A Biography. New York: G.P. Putnam's Sons, 1968, pp. 375, 419.
Williams, John A. Flashbacks. Garden City, N.Y.: Doubleday, 1974, pp. 330, 346.

INTERVIEWS RICH IN BIOGRAPHICAL MATERIAL

Nick Aaron Ford. "He Writes Novel at 20." Afro American Section, October 30, 1948, p. 5.
"Author at Twenty." Our World, vol. 4, no. 1 (January 1949), pp. 40-42.
Jeanne Parot. "Malheur aux Justes." Le Club Francais du Livre, 1952.
Joseph Barry. "An American in Paris-II." New York Post, March 25, 1959, p. 36.
___. "An American in Paris-III." March 26, 1959, p. 36.
Joe Hunter. Guest Columnist. "Jack Saunders SAYS." Philadelphia Tribune, September 23, 1967, p. 8.
Jack Saunders. "Jack Saunders SAYS." Philadelphia Tribune, December 2, 1967, p. 8.
Herbert Lottman. "The Action Is Everywhere the Black Man Goes." New York Times Book Review, April 12, 1968, pp. 6-7, 48-49.
Joseph Bevans Bush. "On Re-Calling William Gardner Smith: Writer and Friend." Philadelphia Tribune, August 30, 1977, p. 21.

ARTICLES ON VARIOUS EVENTS OF SMITH'S CAREER

Jack Conroy. "Negro Soldier and Fraulein." Chicago Sun Times, August 17, 1948.
Bill Bedell. "Two New Stories of Unusual Fiction Merit." Houston Post, August 22, 1948.
Barry Bingham. "Tragedy in Black and White." Courier Journal (Louisville), August 22, 1948.
Wambly Bald. "Young Man Tackles Great Irony." New York Post, August 23, 1948.
Harrison Smith. "Land of Freedom?" Saturday Review of Literature, August 28, 1948, pp. 14-15.
Rita Ochman. "Negro Pens War Novel of Service in Germany." Cleveland Plain Dealer, August 29, 1948.
David Dempsey. "American Dilemma, Army Model." New York Times Book Review, September 5, 1948, p. 6.
"People Who Read and Write." New York Times Book Review, September 5, 1948, p. 10.
Wilbur Needham. "Hammer & Tongs: Negroes in Germany Face Big Problem." Los Angeles, California News, September 11, 1948.
Lisa Aversa. "Temple U. Student Publishes Thought-Provoking 1st Book." Pennsylvania News, October 1948.
Otto Von Zarek. "Ich Aber Kehre Nach Deutschland Zuruck. . . ." Munchner Kulturpressedienst, October 9, 1948.
Ann L. Goodman. "A Novelist on His Own Novel." New York Star, October 21, 1948.
"In Brief." Crisis, November 1948, pp. 346-47.

"Last of the Conquerors." *Negro Digest*, November 1948, pp. 89-94.
"ticker tape: Light on the Literati." *Negro Digest*, November 1948, p. 51.
"Walk in Darkness." *Crisis*, December 1948, p. 379.
"Acceptance as a Human Being." *Phylon*, vol. X, no. 1 (First Quarter 1949), pp. 96-97.
Dorothy McDonald. "The Mail Bag." *Negro Digest*, February 1949, p. 97.
Arthur B. Spingarn. "Books by Negro Authors in 1948." *Crisis*, February 1949, pp. 45-46.
"Smith's War on 'Best List.'" *Philadelphia Tribune*, March 3, 1949, p. 4.
"Bill Smith's Best Seller on 25¢ List." *Pittsburgh Courier*, March 12, 1949, p. 29.
"W. Gardner Smith: Last of the Conquerors." *Times Literary Supplement*, March 12, 1949.
"ticker tape: Light on the Literati." *Negro Digest*, March 1949, p. 50.
"ticker tape: Light on the Literati." *Negro Digest*, June 1949, p. 50.
"Mary Sewell, Young Author Wed in Phila." *Pittsburgh Courier*, July 30, 1949, p. 1.
Alain Locke. "Wisdom de Profundis: The Literature of the Negro, 1949." *Phylon*, vol. X, no. 1 (First Quarter 1950), pp. 5-14, especially p. 9.
George S. Schuyler. "Whats Wrong with Negro Authors." *Negro Digest*, May 1950, pp. 3-7.
Will Thomas. "Negro Writers of Pulp Fiction." *Negro Digest*, July 1950, pp. 81-84.
Nick Aaron Ford, "A Blueprint for Negro Authors," *Phylon*, vol. XI, no. 4. (Fourth Quarter 1950) pp. 374-77, especially p. 374.
Alain Locke. "Inventory at Mid-Century: A Review of the Literature of the Negro for 1950." *Phylon*, vol. XII, no. 1 (First Quarter 1951), pp. 5-12, especially p. 12.
Arthur B. Spingarn. "Books by Negro Authors, 1950." *Crisis*, February 1955, pp. 80, 83.
William Gardner Smith: Anger at Innocence." *Times Literary Supplement*, April 27, 1951, p. 257.
Richard Gibson. "A No to Nothing." *Kenyon Review*, Spring 1951, pp. 252-55.
Doris Dungill Holmes. "Story of Any Negro." *Phlyon*, vol. XVI, no. 1 (First Quarter 1955), pp. 115-17.
Blyden Jackson. "The Blithe Newcomers." *Phylon*, vol. XVI, no. 1 (First Quarter 1955), pp. 5-12, especially p 9.
Arthur B. Spingarn. "Books by Negro Authors, 1954." *Crisis*, February 1955, pp. 83, 87.
Henry F. Winslow, "High Fidelity." *Crisis*, February 1955, pp. 124-25.
"Amid the Alien Corn." *Time*, November 17, 1958, p. 28.
"The Stone Face." *Crisis*, December 1963, p. 635.
Jean Carey Bond. "Excellent Ideas in Search of Greater Skill." *Freedomways*, vol. IV, no. 2 (Spring 1964), pp. 272-74.

"The Lost Generation Meets it Epigoni." *Paris Gazette*, May 24-May 30, 1964.

Nick Aaron Ford. "The Fire Next Time?" A Critical Survey of Belle Lettres By and About Negroes Published in 1963." *Phylon*. vol. XXV, no. 2 (Summer 1964), pp. 124-26.

"Then and Now." *Paris Review*, vol. IX, no. 33 (Winter-Spring, 1965), pp. 158-70. Panel discussion of expatriates of the 1920s and expatriates of the 1950s and 1960s held at the American Students' and Artists' Center, Paris, in the spring of 1964.

Mary Goodfellow and Toni Howard. "Ex-Philadelphian Is Critical of the West." *Evening Bulletin* (Philadelphia), October 14, 1965.

Jerry H. Bryant. "Individuality and Fraternity: The Novels of William Gardner Smith." *Studies in Black Literature*, vol. III, no. 2 (Summer 1972), pp. 1-8.

Arthur Orrmont. "Editing in the '40s, Or, Flung from the Ivory Tower." *Connecticut Review*, vol. VIII, no. 1 (October 1973), pp. 6-15.

Stanley Schatt. "You Must Go Home Again: Today's Afro-American Expatriate Writers." *Negro American Literature Forum*, vol. 7 no. 3 (Fall 1973), pp. 80-82.

Obituary Notices

"William G. Smith, U.S. Journalist in France, Dies." *International Herald-Tribune*, November 7, 1974.

"Bill Smith." *Le Monde*, November 8, 1974, p. 27.

"William Gardner Smith, Author and Newspaperman, Dies at 47." *New York Times*, November 8, 1974, p. 42.

"W. J. Smith, Journalist and Author." *Washington Post*, November 8, 1974, p. C10.

"Writer Dies in France." *New York Amsterdan News*, November 16, 1974, p. C1.

"Black Author, Journalist Dies in Paris Hospital." *Jet*, November 28, 1974, p. 16.

"William Gardner Smith." *Black World*, February 1975, p. 97.

Index

About the Author

LeROY S. HODGES, JR., received the Doctorat de l'Université de Paris from the Sorbonne Nouvelle. He has taught at New York City (Community) Technical College, New York Institute of Technology, Adelphi University, and The City College of the City University of New York. Born in Brooklyn, New York, Dr. Hodges is currently researching a notable personality of modern Afro-American history.

Recent Titles in
Contributions in Afro-American and African Studies
Series Advisers: John W. Blassingame and Henry Louis Gates, Jr.

Voices from Under: Black Narrative in Latin America and the Caribbean
William Luis, editor

Contemporary Public Policy Perspectives and Black Americans: Issues in an Era of Retrenchment Politics
Mitchell F. Rice and Woodrow Jones, Jr., editors

Student Culture and Activism in Black South African Universities: The Roots of Resistance
Mokubung O. Nkomo

The Cinema of Ousmane Sembene, A Pioneer of African Film
Françoise Pfaff

Philanthropy and Jim Crow in American Social Science
John H. Stanfield

Israel in the Black American Perspective
Robert G. Weisbord and Richard Kazarian, Jr.

African Culture: The Rhythms of Unity
Molefi Kete Asante and Kariamu Welsh Asante, editors

Writing "Independent" History: African Historiography, 1960–1980
Caroline Neale

More Than Drumming: Essays on African and Afro-Latin American Music and Musicians
Irene V. Jackson, editor

More Than Dancing: Essays on Afro-American Music and Musicians
Irene V. Jackson, editor

Sterling A. Brown: Building the Black Aesthetic Tradition
Joanne V. Gabbin

Amalgamation!: Race, Sex, and Rhetoric in the Nineteenth-Century American Novel
James Kinney

CPSIA information can be obtained
at www.ICGtesting.com
Printed in the USA
BVHW040147060619
550302BV00010B/70/P

9 780313 248825